THE

The Cresset Library

The Best Circles
Leonore Davidoff

Britain by Mass Observation
Arranged and written by Tom Harrison and Charles Madge

China: A Short Cultural History
C. P. Fitzgerald

From Ploughtail to Parliament
An autobiography
Joseph Arch

A Short History of Ireland
J. C. Beckett

Wittgenstein
W. W. Bartley III

Cover: *Hush!* by James Tissot
Courtesy of The City Art Gallery, Manchester

LEONORE DAVIDOFF

The Best Circles

SOCIETY ETIQUETTE
AND THE SEASON

NEW INTRODUCTION BY
VICTORIA GLENDINNING

THE CRESSET LIBRARY

London   Melbourne   Sydney   Auckland   Johannesburg

The Cresset Library

An imprint of Century Hutchinson Ltd

62–65 Chandos Place, London WC2N 4NW

Century Hutchinson Publishing Group (Australia) Pty Ltd
16–22 Church Street, Hawthorn, Melbourne, Victoria 3122

Century Hutchinson Group (NZ) Ltd
32–34 View Road, PO Box 40–086, Glenfield, Auckland 10

Century Hutchinson (SA) (Pty) Ltd
PO Box 337, Bergvlei 2012, South Africa

First published 1973 by Croom Helm Ltd
This edition first published 1986

Printed and bound in Great Britain by
Richard Clay (The Chaucer Press) Ltd, Bungay, Suffolk

British Library Cataloguing in Publication Data

Davidoff, Leonore
    The best circles.—(The Cresset library; 2)
    1. Upper classes—Great Britain—History
    2. Great Britain—Social life and customs
    I. Title
    941.081   DA533

ISBN 0 09 168761 6

CONTENTS

· ❀ ·

INTRODUCTION TO
THE CRESSET LIBRARY EDITION

—————————— · ❁ · ——————————

This is a book about upper-class women – perhaps I should say ladies – and how they controlled and regulated social life and social contacts in Victorian and Edwardian England. We are perhaps too quick to think of all nineteenth- and early twentieth-century women as the oppressed victims of a male-dominated society. That is the conventional feminist view – and of course there were thousands of bored, unhappy girls and women, unfitted to the only career open to them, whose intelligence and aspirations were wasted and frustrated.

But those who wholeheartedly embraced the career of marriage to a prosperous and prominent man and entered 'Society', at whatever level, found themselves with a demanding whole-time job. In the very best of the 'best circles', political hostesses had real influence on affairs of state. It was in a social setting that alliances were formed and decisions informally taken, and social life was run by women, its leaders and 'filters'. Even in the new streets of suburban villas, as Leonore Davidoff describes, bourgeois ladies formed their exclusive circles and could decide to cold-shoulder some families and promote the fortunes of others. All the energy and ingenuity of the female sex could be exploited in this subtle form of social control; not the least of its purposes was to see that the younger generation met only 'suitable' mates.

The idea behind *The Best Circles*, then, is that social activities which sound to us just crazily complicated ways of using up time and money were, in fact, highly functional. Most ladies did not feel they were wasting their time paying morning calls, giving 'At Homes', chaperoning their daughters at balls, working out who should go down to dinner with whom, and whether or not they should bow to Mrs X when they met her on the street. This was their work, and their duty. The 'primacy of social goals' for such women, in a moral rather than a materialistic sense, is one of Dr Davidoff's chief discoveries – though it is perhaps the confusion of morality with feelings of social superiority that the modern reader finds most offensive in Victorian values.

The Best Circles first appeared in 1973, before 'women's studies' was a common phrase in this country, and before writing and publishing books for women, by women, and about women and their history had become as familiar to the general reader as it is today. The book stands out now, as it did in 1973, because it is as readable, as clear, and as cleverly illustrated as many a lighter work, while being based on solid academic research. But it is not only a book for women, but for anyone fascinated by the domestic and social detail of the past and by the broad sweep of changing fashions and trends. It is a book about how a certain set of people behaved; and some of the ritualized social behaviour which came under the heading of 'etiquette' seems now ridiculous and incredible.

Dr Davidoff is a sociologist, which gives her historical writing its particular tone. She defines 'Society' as 'a system of quasi-kinship relationships which was used to "place" mobile individuals' in a period when industrialization, new money, and the population shift from country to city were making upheavals in the social system. Networks of 'quasi-kinship relationships', as she observes, are as important in the East End as in Belgravia; forming such networks is part of being human. But the tribal customs of the rich, the well-bred, and the influential developed to a point of baroque ritual impossible for other classes in the decades she is considering.

In the late 1960s and early 1970s, many of us felt that Britain was becoming, or could become, a 'classless society'. This has not happened. One odd result of our currently stratified society is that the formal hierarchies described in this book actually seem rather less extraordinary to me now than they did when I first read it in 1973.

With perspective, one can even see the thin residue of the activities described in *The Best Circles* still in operation in 1986. Historical periods and patterns of behaviour do not have neat cut-offs, like slices of bread; they leak into one another, both backwards and forwards. There would still, in the mid nineteenth century, have been dowagers who embarrassed their demure Victorian grandchildren by the frank manner and crude speech of the more robust eighteenth century. And there are plenty of ladies in their seventies and eighties around today who experienced the Season very much as Dr Davidoff describes it in this book; the last batch of debutantes to be presented at Court (though not wearing a train and feathers, after the Second World War) are still only in their forties. There are still political dinner-parties, and country-house parties, and coming-out parties, and annual Charity Balls organized by groups of rich friends. No one who reads 'Jennifer's Diary' in *Harpers & Queen* could doubt that for some people at least it is very much business as usual so far as Society is concerned.

There are important differences, though. The massive infrastructure of permanent staff – butler, footmen, parlourmaids, housemaids, cook, laundrywoman etc. – has been seriously eroded even for the seriously wealthy. 'Society' has become infinitely more complex and flexible, too. The concept originated as a means of excluding the undesirable, for any system of classing and categorizing is a system of exclusion. The old world of the landed aristocracy may have lost its political clout, and numerically it has always been insignificant. But the Royal Family is more glittery than ever, and style-watchers constantly identify new social in-groups – Sloanes and Yuppies are the obvious examples. The English mania for socially classifying ourselves and others seems undiminished.

Simply, there are more kinds of intersecting 'best circles' today; not only the network of the old gentry, but the worlds of politics, big business, the City, theatre, the arts, television, sport and so on all have their hierarchies, and the top dogs from each are more likely to meet one another socially than they are to meet those on the lower echelons of their own world.

I have a book called *Manners and Rules of Good Society* by an unnamed 'Member of the Aristocracy', published in 1898, which is designed for upwardly mobile and ambitious families. It is full of warnings about the shameful consequences of making social solecisms. Its author cannot envisage Society without visiting-cards:

> The etiquette of card-leaving and that of paying calls are indisputably necessary. Without these aids to order and method all intercourse between friends and acquaintances would be uncertain and chaotic.

Uncertainty and chaos, of course, was what the old order most feared. But one of the reasons why we have never had a revolution in this country since the 1640s is that 'Society' was open-ended. By acquiring the right social skills, and the right income, and the right house, and well-trained servants, anyone could join: hence the proliferation of etiquette handbooks towards the end of the century, to help the nouveaux riches to conform. By making it possible for a successful northern manufacturer, for example, to see his grandchildren as 'gentlemen', some of the seeds of dissent were scattered to the wind. Traditional 'Society', by making it feasible, but not *too* easy, for outsiders to join its ranks, was instinctively prolonging its own hegemony. Stability was maintained. So were gross inequalities, piously accepted by all but radical thinkers as part of the natural law.

Even this mechanism is evident today. It is natural for parents to want 'the best' for their children, and the 'primacy of social goals' is still there for many people. The public schools – also developed in the nineteenth century to groom the young to meet Society's demands – are doing well, and many of their pupils are the children of fathers who were not themselves educated at a public school. The ideal of the 'country gentleman' is alive and well too: business men (those 'in trade' as the Victorians would say dismissively) lose no time when they have made their pile in acquiring a Georgian house in the shires and spending their weekends in green wellies, a labrador at their side, tramping their acres.

And why not? The ideal of the country gentleman is a very pleasant one. And even some servants in a great country house or Mayfair mansion in the nineteenth century were not necessarily unhappy.* Life was exciting, in the Season; and even if they worked long hours, they had regular meals provided, and a home, and companionship, in an age when there was not safety net of social security and only the workhouse to fall back on. The more we learn about anything, the less we find ourselves able to make snap judgements.

The Best Circles is a good read; it is a book to enjoy. But however amazed, and amused, and even shocked we may be by the elaborate rituals of Society, etiquette and the Season, it's no good thinking that it has nothing to do with us, or that Britain in the 1980s is somehow unrelated to Britain in the 1880s. As Leonore Davidoff writes in her final paragraph: 'In the present climate of uncertainty about the relationships of individuals to larger units of society and the family in particular, it is vital to have some understanding of what has gone before.'

Victoria Glendinning
1986

* Dr Davidoff qualifies this view in her article, 'Mastered for life: servant and wife in Victorian and Edwardian England', in A. Sutcliffe and P. Thane, *Essays in Social History II* (Oxford University Press 1986).

LIST OF ILLUSTRATIONS

·❄·

For my parents

IDA F. DAVIDOFF
LEO M. DAVIDOFF

'There are only two crimes in Society: one to be
poor, the other to be found out.'

Mrs Alec Tweedie
Thirteen Years of a Busy Woman's Life
1912

PREFACE

————— · ❊ · —————

This short volume is intended to be part of a wider study of domestic life and household management in Victorian and Edwardian Britain. It provides a framework for more detailed investigation. This does not mean, however, that it cannot be considered as an analysis in its own right; only that some of the statements are made at a general level. It is, indeed, more in the nature of an introductory essay and as such will, I hope, provoke some discussion on methods of investigation as well as substantive findings.

My first acknowledgement must be to the Fellows and members of Lucy Cavendish College, Cambridge, who by their encouragement made it possible for me to start on the study of Victorian and Edwardian domestic life. The project has been financially supported throughout by the Nuffield Foundation; my particular grant being under the friendly sponsorship of Dr Kenneth Blyth.

In the writing of the book I owe a special debt to Professor J. A. Banks, University of Leicester, for his advice and enthusiasm. My work has also benefited from discussions with Professor David Chaplin, University of Western Michigan, Dr Brian Harrison, Corpus Christi College, Oxford, and Dr Cynthia White, City of London Polytechnic. Discussions with my colleagues at the University of Essex, Dr Paul Thompson, Colin Bell and Howard Newby have given me many insights into the problems of combining historical and sociological research.

I have had invaluable aid from various libraries and Record Offices and would like to thank the many librarians and archivists who unstintingly give so much time and thought to helping with documentary research. In particular I would like to thank Mr Terry Tostevin and the staff of the University of Essex Library, Miss Surrey at the Women's Service Library and A. N. L. Munby of King's College, Cambridge, who allowed me to use his private collection of books on household management and etiquette.

Last, but certainly not least, I would like to thank June Freeman and Fiona Rudd for all their patient support during the writing of this book. Of course there is no question that the final responsibility for the work is mine alone.

CHAPTER I

·✸·

Introduction

The ideas put forward in this book are the result of an academic serendipity. In the course of research into other areas of British nineteenth- and twentieth-century social and economic life (women's employment, domestic service and household management) patterns of both ideal and actual behaviour began to emerge which were puzzling to a mid-twentieth-century observer. Other investigators, too, have raised related questions. For example, Banks convincingly argues that in the third quarter of the nineteenth century the middle classes began to limit family size in order to maintain the 'paraphernalia of gentility' which had so greatly expanded in the preceding decades.[1] Housekeeping manuals, etiquette books and magazines of the period confirm that the expected standard of living had risen considerably for all upper- and middle-class groups. Much of the expenditure was, however, on items of ceremonial display and formal entertainment within the home. One of the largest items was undoubtedly for personal services and the household establishment necessary to maintain these services. This raises the question of why the wealth was spent in this way.

Then there is the problem of the middle-class adulation of the country gentleman ideal and the absence of a truly urban, bourgeois life-style. W. J. Reader has asked why, with all their technical knowledge and commitment to a scientific ethos, professional men did not try to reform the anti-scientific curriculum of the public schools.[2] He speculates that it must have been the 'dual character of their ambition'. Where did this ambition originate? Why did it have such authority in the face of conflicting ideals?

There is also a collection of descriptive material about Victorian middle-class women and their sequestration in the home, with its corollary emphasis on respectability through control of sexual behaviour. Undoubtedly the quality of life this produced for many women was psychologically stultifying. Why were there so few alternatives available to them? And when alternatives did present themselves, why were they so loath to follow them?[3] The descriptions of women's lives and Victorian family life are generally presented as quaint anecdotes about our forebears, which give few satisfactory answers, much less ask relevant questions.[4] Yet we know that the economic consequences of the doctrine which confined women to the home were disastrous for many middle- and working-class families. For this reason alone it is worthwhile to attempt a more sophisticated analysis.

In addition to the anecdotal approach to women's affairs, there has been a perhaps unjustified emphasis on unusual women and unusual activities: feminine path-breakers, women writers and the Suffrage movement. It is surely as important to look at the social and domestic lives of the majority of Victorians, both men and women, in the context of their other commitments and activities.

The missing pieces to most of the puzzle seem to fall into place if account is taken of the system of organising social and domestic life which began to be codified in the 1820s under the rubric Society and its accompanying calendar of events, the Season.[5] A Society of sorts had existed before that time on a national level at least, centring around the Court, but the system was vastly expanded and infused with new authority in the second quarter of the century. It flourished from then on for about 120 years reaching ever wider social and geographic circles. Modern commentators, who refer to the system only in passing, have misunderstood and underestimated its importance. For example, Gillian Avery, a perceptive analyst of Victorian social life, says of the late Victorian period: 'It was an era when the upper-class middle-aged woman had erected a vast structure of time-consuming devices to conceal from herself how much time she had on her hands.'[6] If sociology has no other virtue, it should alert us to be wary of an explanation like this, which assumes that large numbers of people living far above a poverty line would have continued to accept, much less passionately defend, a system which was without meaning and without goals.

It is true that writers like W. L. Guttsman[7] and F. M. L. Thompson[8] have noted that London Society was effective in furthering the amalgamation of new wealth with the existing elite. Their interest has been from a political and economic viewpoint[9] whereas this study will look at Society in detail as a linking factor *between* the family and political and economic institutions. As such it proved to be an extremely flexible mechanism, useful to social groups faced with the consequences of increased population and urban growth, industrial development and political realignment which were the characteristics of the first half of the century.

A study of this kind bridges the disciplines of sociology and history and I realise that in an introductory work such as this, neither historians nor sociologists may be satisfied, but this is unavoidable. The period covered, nearly one hundred and fifty years, is too long, and the area, virtually the whole of the British Isles, is too large, to allow for more than the following brief sketch. Much more detailed research would be needed to fill in the outlines.

Sociologically, Society can be seen as a system of quasi-kinship relationships which was used to 'place' mobile individuals during the period of structural differentiation fostered by industrialisation and urbanisation. As such it can be understood as a feature of a community based on common claims to status honour which were in turn based on a certain life-style. In this historical case such claims were defined as attributes of English *ladies* and *gentlemen*. Like all status groups, the traditional aristocratic elite were obsessively concerned with the question of access to their ranks. New market conditions created a body of people making claims to social recognition as well as the political recognition of 1832 and 1867. As Weber says in a general analysis of such claims:

> If mere economic acquisition and naked economic power still bearing the stigma of its extra-status origin could bestow upon anyone who has won it the same honor as those who are interested in status by virtue of style of life claim for themselves, the status order would be threatened at its very root. This is the more so as, given equality of status honor, property *per se* represents an addition even if it is not overtly acknowledged as such. Yet if such economic acquisition and power gave the agent any honor at all, his wealth would result in his attaining more honor than those who successfully claim honor by virtue of style of life.[10]

Under the impact of industrialisation, new forms of wealth as well as newly wealthy groups produced a flood of applicants that threatened to overwhelm the life-style itself. The strictly structured access rituals of nineteenth-century Society and etiquette must be seen in this context.

Modern sociologists, partly because of their ahistorical bias, have usually tended to see leadership of such groups as exercised informally. Kadushin, in explaining his idea of the 'social circle' says:

> The major informal mechanism which links power persons and power organisations is the social circle: the exact counterpart on the social system level of the informal shop system at the organisational level.[11]

But Society in the nineteenth century, especially in England, did become formalised. One way of formalising a social institution is to use specialised personnel to carry out its functions. In nineteenth-century England upper- and middle-class women were used to maintain the fabric of Society, as semi-official leaders but also as arbiters of social acceptance or rejection. By effectively preventing upper- and middle-class women from playing any part in the market,[12] any part in public life whatsoever, the Victorians believed that one section of the population would be able to provide a haven of stability, of exact social classification in the threatening anonymity of the surrounding economic and political upheaval.

Two further important sociological points must be made about Great Britain in this period. Although it was a time of great economic and political turmoil, there was no real external threat despite continuing fears of invasion from various quarters. The one hundred years of peace, 1815 to 1914, indeed of vast economic and administrative expansion overseas, allowed time for the system to mature gradually without the sudden breaks of war; a situation always favourable to the consolidation of status honour by elite groups.

Secondly, Great Britain was nationally a unit, ethnically a remarkably homogeneous country. With the exception of ever-rebellious Catholic Ireland, the 'Celtic fringe' had not only been militarily conquered several generations before, but its elites had become intertwined by marriage, education, language and culture with that of the dominant English majority.[13] (The great Catholic families were English, the Irish aristocracy were predominantly Protestant.) Such a homogeneous group, freed from external threats or constraints developed a life-style which clearly demonstrated to the indigenous working class and the outside world its claim to status honour and which at the same time generated an intense feeling of community among its members despite their geographic spread over a wide area.

Looking at the problem from a historian's point of view, the shift from a society where patronage and familial or client relationship were the norm to a system where individual achievement was rewarded with great wealth and power, was bewildering to those living through the change.[14] Increased geographical mobility through better transport also disrupted received notions of social placing.[15] In contradistinction to these chaotic new developments, the rules of Society and the confining of social life to private homes made possible the minute regulation of personal daily life.[16] It also made possible the evaluation and placing of newcomers in the social landscape. It legitimated the break with kin and the neglect of kinship interaction when these became incompatible with social mobility and in some cases even provided a network of pseudo-kin as replacements. Finally, the filtering of personnel through the sieve of Society regulated access to political power, economic position and the accumulation of capital.

Gradually these functions were taken over by other institutions. Political office at all levels became elective; professional and civil service appointments were open to competitive examination; the public schools became recognised as a necessary adjunct to middle- and upper-class life-style.[17] The more theatrical and hedonistic functions of Society were then emphasised, and the 'marriage market' became its surviving claim to serious attention. Inevitably this meant that more activities were performed by the young, and the regulation of Society events turned over primarily to women. Consequently it has come to appear 'trivialised' in the eyes of historical analysts. It is only one complete generation since even this attenuated Society ceased to have significant influence in daily life for the upper and middle class. Perhaps it is only now that we can begin to see it more objectively.

It should be understood that the rules of Society and etiquette as described in this study were no more than a blueprint of expectations and that human beings reacted to them in a variety of ways. Even in upper-class circles, very few of the participants realised what the system was as a whole or what functions it performed. They accepted its rubrics because they were 'the right thing to do', i.e., they were norms which had been thoroughly internalised and legitimised and, for those who voluntarily defined themselves within the orbit of

Society, they were binding. Viscountess Rhondda looking back on her two Seasons after coming out says:

> Yet I do not remember that I consciously criticised a system which was responsible for persuading a particularly affectionate and conscientious mother (who if left to please herself would have desired to spend three-quarters of her time either painting miniatures or working in her garden and the other quarter in an old furniture shop) that she could best do her duty by martyrising herself into dragging a bored and not even socially successful daughter through a series of aimless and useless functions. A system which hypnotised a perfectly intelligent, though perhaps rather a naive young woman, already anxious to investigate most accepted notions impersonally and dispassionately, into acceding without question to indulgence in this odd form of occupation, which in fact she was hating so much.[18]

Most people only came into contact with a part of the system, especially those living quiet provincial lives on a modest income. But my aim is to present a picture of the total system and some of its consequences for other institutions in the society. The blueprint of Society outlined here, then, is not a complete picture of social reality, but is a description of the framework of constraints within which individuals and familes lived out their lives.

SOURCES

Caution must be exercised in using sources such as housekeeping books, manuals of etiquette and the advice columns in magazines as evidence of existing attitudes and behaviour. These publications often seem to be sheer fantasy-peddling for profit, and yet the number turned out from the 1830s onwards indicates that they were fulfilling a need for social guidance.[19] Something of the same caveat should be followed in making fiction a source for sociological analysis. The most useful balance to these sources is in personal memory which can be tapped by diaries, autobiographies and where possible personal interviews. I have been able to examine about one hundred and fifty middle- and upper-class and fifty domestic servant 'memories'.[20] Very often the period covered goes back to the author's parents or grandparents so that the period c. 1820 to c. 1950 is represented. Most of these were written as family history or because of contacts with well-known personalities so that the evidence on social and domestic life is usually presented simply as it was experienced by the author. Although only a selected few of these books and interviews can be cited in the text, all of them provide the basis of the argument throughout the study.

CHAPTER II

· ❊ ·

Society and The Season
in the
Nineteenth Century

Eighteenth-century society was small. Mingay estimates that about three to four hundred made up the total of the greatest families. These included some wealthy merchants and bankers but mostly landowners 'whose wealth, influence and style of living distinguished them from the inferior ranks of landed society and enabled them to support a great house and employ it as a centre of social and political influence'.[1] The great town houses like Bedford House and Devonshire House were the centres of political activity. Their owners' corresponding county seats served as centres of local politics.[2] John Summerson in *Georgian England* describes how the architecture of these great houses enhanced the public quality of social life. They had 'immense public rooms and small squalid back bedrooms. They were not built for domestic but for public life—a life of continued entertaining in drawing rooms, ante-rooms and "eating rooms" where conversation would not be wholly ephemeral, where a sentence might be delivered which would echo round political England, where an introduction might mean the beginning of a career or a deft criticism, the dethronement of a policy.'[3]

The English aristocracy and gentry have always been hierarchical yet fluid with family mobility in both directions. Primogeniture and entailment have always meant that there has been a supply of younger sons to take up careers in the armed services, the church and the law. Although these occupations were followed in a manner that allowed time for other gentlemanly pursuits, sooner or later they usually did necessitate leaving the family seat and moving into a wider environment.

In the early nineteenth century more of these sons—and their sisters—survived. There were plenty of titled and untitled upper-class young men to fill the expanding positions of an economically buoyant society. At this time also, landed proprietors were willing to exploit new sources of income in agriculture, in mineral rights or rents from new building on their urban land holdings. Thus, even in the remotest part of the country the great landed families tended to be an active elite, albeit often on a local scale. But they were active in politics and estate management in a leisurely way. Their social life was part of their governance and was equally joined by men and women.

An important factor in the continued dominance of this group was the lack of legal as well as social barriers to ennoblement and the fact that ennoblement was not a necessary prelude to political activity.[4] The untitled gentry, on the one hand an intermediate group with ties to the nobility by marriage and similar life-styles, on the other linked by family ties and farming interest to farmers and the middle class, has long been recognised as a crucial factor in the English social hierarchy. The difference which these facts made in expectations and loyalties is striking by contrast with French experience where not only were there legal and customary blockages to commercial and professional groups seeking entry to the aristocracy, but also similar disincentives for members of the aristocracy to take up commercial or professional careers despite government encouragement.[5] In England, it will be seen how formalised Society took the place of mobility controlled through legal classifications. By regulating yet allowing the flow of new personnel, it prevented the formation of angry, alienated newcomer groups barred from full social recognition.

When new wealthy families began to consolidate their positions in growing numbers in the first quarter of the nineteenth century, the domination of both town and country, capital city and hinterland by the elite was already almost complete.[6] The leading families of the counties made the annual pilgrimage to London to attend the 'greatest club of all', Parliament. In August, when the stench of the uncleansed Thames forced them to leave, they returned to their county seats to direct the local government of the counties through the network of their smaller neighbours and lesser relations. This seasonal migration, which was only possible because of the small size of the island, was a crucial factor in the continuing hold of these groups over the leadership of a society undergoing such rapid changes.

The middle classes of merchants, manufacturers, professional men and tradesmen who were to be found for the most part in cities and small towns accepted the leadership of the landed gentry. Such middle groups, however, were in more immediate contact with the problems of rapid population growth and urbanisation. As Asa Briggs vividly describes, they feared the chaos in the expanding cities where the lower classes no longer knew their place, where they themselves were as likely to fall 'into the abyss' as to become wealthy new men.[7]

The slow growth of new wealth from reorganised farming methods and the new textile industries was accelerated by fortunes made in the Napoleonic War. The response to such changes by individuals and groups varied with their geographical and social location. For example, although the tendency was for tenants of large farms to emulate the gentry in their social life as prosperity increased,[8] some chose to remain working farmers. Their recreations were local sporting and agricultural events. Why did others choose to try going into Society? As in the case of the newly rich manufacturers 'a socially ambitious wife or a son educated at public school often effected the change'.[9] But this is a question that needs further research.

Whatever the cause, there is no doubt that in the 1830s and 1840s there was a reinterpretation of the idea of Society and the expectations for individual behaviour to gain access to that society. Under these pressures, an increasing division between public and private life was stressed. New importance was placed on privacy for upper- and middle-class family and social life.[10] Many farmhouses were renovated to create a private sitting-room separate from the living kitchen, especially in the south where the custom of giving farm servants bed and board was dying out. There were social as well as physical fears of new and more rapid travel. In the 1830s the wife of a country gentleman had her own coach put on the railway car as 'it was impossible for her to travel in a rail road carriage as she might find herself sitting opposite someone with whom she was not acquainted'.[11] And Girouard notes that while Regency and Georgian great houses were open to the public, some even having printed guide books for the visitor, Victorian gentlemen regarded their homes not as a temple to taste but to domestic virtues,[12] one of which was engaging in Society functions.

At the beginning of the century, besides the great town and country houses, the other meeting places of the elite had been similarly public, for example the pleasure gardens of Ranleagh, Vauxhall and Hampstead Wells which were closed or abandoned by the upper and middle classes during the middle years of the nineteenth century. 'Private as opposed to public drinking was becoming a sign of respectability'.[13] A commentator looking back from 1871 noticed:

> that they [the very great] should partake of these pleasures in company that was always mixed and sometimes more than dubious as to its quality, supping, dancing and playing at cards and hazard in the close proximity to very queer folks indeed is stranger still . . . and yet to the best of our knowledge no special harm or annoyance appears to have resulted from this singular comingling of the classes.[14]

He goes on to speculate quite correctly that this mixing may have been possible because barriers of rank and station 'were more respected then'.

Several other changes in early nineteenth-century social life indicate that problems of social definition were becoming more acute. For example what started as a set of subscription dances open to the purchase of tickets, at a club, Almacks, was slowly taken over by a powerful coterie of patronesses, like Lady Castlereagh and Lady Jersey, who began to apply extremely strict criteria for entry and behaviour until eventually tales were being circulated that even the Duke of Wellington was turned away for being five minutes late.[15] Whether this was true or not, such stories show how attempts at closure by certain groups were attracting interest. At this period, masquerade balls were still being held and adventuresses like Harriette Wilson could still attend public functions where Society gathered.[16] The last such ball at the end of a brilliant 1818 season was at Burlington House where 1,600 people danced. Jugglers, a lottery, cards and masked dancing were included in what could as well be described as a public carouse. But such public entertainments, where masks helped to hide social identity, were falling into disfavour. The new sober mood after the Napoleonic War furthered their decline. By the 1820s and 1830s, in London Society at any rate, there are hints that many houses of great hostesses which were still fairly lax in defining social acceptability were only attended by men.

Just after its inauguration in 1841, *Punch* ran a monthly series of sketches called 'The Side Scenes of Society' chronicling the social adventures of an unattractively 'nouveau riche' family, the Spangle

Lacquers. The resentment here seems to be against their use of public places to try to gain access to private domains.

> You will always be certain to meet at the Lacquers' a great many persons with whom you are perfectly well acquainted by sight, but to whom you can assign no fixed position in society, having generally met them in places where distinction was acquired by paying for it. You will see them sailing up the avenues of a morning concert—they cross your pathway in going to their carriages from Howell and James's; they brush against you at the conclusion of the performances at the opera.[17]

This was also the period when London clubs grew in numbers and influence. It is true that the increase was in part a response to the need for somewhere to stay in London for less wealthy gentlemen who were now coming to town more frequently. But it was also part of the general growth of semi-private institutions where rules of selectivity would guarantee social acceptability. In the 1870s when criteria of selection had relaxed to allow some professional men to membership (barristers, physicians, clergy and the armed services but not surgeons and architects) but not yet businessmen, a club habitué wrote, 'the fundamental character of the perfect club ought to be an unassuming unobtrusive and unenvious equality'.[18] The club provided the same kind of social protection as the private home[19] without the rigid formality of etiquette imposed by women or the financial burden of upkeep. Clubs made it possible for the unattached man to continue to operate in the social sphere without maintaining his own establishment and in this way encouraged the late marriage age for men which was a feature of mid-Victorian life.

These developments towards greater exclusiveness, privacy and controlled social interaction took place against a background of certain stable elements in social life. The most important of these was the protocol surrounding the Court.[20] Historically the Court was considered to be the greatest house among very many great houses. Because of this, access to the Court was essentially the same as for any private house. It was necessary to have a personal introduction through an individual sponsor, usually but not always a relative, who had already been accepted within the royal circle. This individual would send cards, his own and his nominee's, in advance. The introduction would then be accepted or rejected. If accepted, the newcomer could then be presented to the Sovereign. These presentations took place at any special change in the prominent person's life. He or she was expected to visit the Sovereign on accession of dignity (i.e. office), matrimony or any kind of social or professional advancement. This was as much to keep the Sovereign informed as to receive his congratulations. Drawing-rooms, where presentations were made, were attended by both men and women and it was here that women were presented both before and after marriage. Marriage was seen for both men and women as a change in status. The young man, for example, was expected to be presented by his *wife's* most important relative to show his new connection at its best. The concentration on young girls being presented for the first time that we associate with twentieth-century 'Society' did not exist.

By mid-century it was becoming clear that being presented to the Queen was already less of a visit among a quasi-family and more of a 'passport to Society'.[21] Certificates of Presentation were first given in 1854 and about that time a manual of instruction for access to the Court appeared. In it the anonymous author complained at what he saw as the privacy, even secretiveness, of the whole procedure.

> It may naturally be considered that ceremonies which require so much care in their superintendence on the part of the Officers of the Crown, which lead to so large an expenditure both of time and money on the part of the visitors, and which exercise so important an influence over the higher circles of British society must have some official or recognised organ of publication— some channel through which the *public at large* can learn who has been presented to the Sovereign, and who has not enjoyed that advantage.[22]

—but no, only by sufferance was the author of the Court Circular, printed by the newspaper, allowed to stand near the windows in the Tapestry Chamber and to copy the cards which had been left on the table of the Queen's page.

State Balls at Buckingham Palace, Royal entertainments and Royal attendance at certain functions gave a stamp of authority to the whole fabric of Society. Those within the Court, for example, the ladies-in-waiting, could give a lead in behaviour or 'take up' new sets of people. Because of this, the contrasting personalities of Queen Victoria and Prince (later King) Edward did make a certain amount of difference in the minutiae of Society life. But for the most part the institution functioned independently of personalities.

In the 1840s the great houses still acted as closed camps for their political party interests. This was typified by Lady Palmerston at Cambridge House. It was said that an invitation to her parties had determined many a wavering vote. She used her favours in strictly a party sense.[23] So closely were parliamentary and social affairs connected that when Parliament was in session many dinner parties were timed to begin when the House rose and members expected to go straight from the debates to the home of their favourite hostess where, along with their coterie of supporters, political discussion continued far into the night. Later, in the 1850s–1870s Lady Waldegrave's reign at Strawberry Hill, her Twickenham home, widened the field of interest and recruitment. Her receptions were open to Whigs, Tories and Radicals, literary figures and very important newspaper editors. She had friends at Court. Her June and July, Friday-to-Monday parties were a significant part of the London Season where Disraeli and Gladstone could be seen to breakfast together. Non-political 'mixers' such as private theatricals and games were some of the pastimes. She also had Wiltshire and Surrey houses which brought the national elites into touch with local affairs.[24]

Although not everyone could be as skilful or as fascinating as Lady Waldegrave, this pattern was repeated in the great country houses dotted over the British Isles.[25]

In a gathering of people selected by a really clever hostess, there might be one or two Cabinet Ministers who welcomed the opportunity of quiet conversation, or there might be a Viceroy or high official from a far-off corner of the Empire, anxious to make someone in the government of the day realise a little more the difficulties of a particular experiment that Britain had delegated to him to carry out. These parties often included a diplomat home on leave, a painter, and almost certainly a musician who played to some of the company in the evenings (she is speaking here of the late Victorian period). Beside these eminent people there was usually a sprinkling of women famous for their beauty or wit or both, who either gave the conversation a sparkling turn, or were wise enough not to interrupt good talk, and who accordingly sat looking statuesque or flowerlike.[26]

This somewhat idealised picture of country house parties remained unchanged over several generations. Often local notables would be asked to attend some of the lesser functions at these gatherings and at the county level country-house dining and visiting opened the way to 'the two symbols of the merger of a new family into the life of county society—i.e., service in the magistry and marriage alliances with county families'.[27] But new wealth which could buy country properties had to work hard socially for these prizes.[28] This interpretation may help to explain why so much emphasis was put on musical and literary entertainment at home. Private concerts and private theatricals flourished at this time, serving as an inducement to important guests; outstanding performers were hired as attractions for evenings at private homes only accessible by private invitation.[29]

The formation of a formal social life confined to private locations and rigidly defined by convention which was embraced by aristocratic and middle classes in both town and country made it possible for upwardly mobile individuals and parts of families to gain access to new groups if they had the necessary qualifications. Before this period, the problem of maintaining barriers against newcomers was never so important. The whole basis of social relations was family (or pseudo-family) ties between equals in the elite, or patronage across well-defined hierarchical lines. The new formalised system of etiquette made it possible, for the first time, to *use* those kin alliances that were profitable and quietly to drop those that were not.[30] And there is evidence that this was widely practised. Society leaders could be used as sponsors in place of kin if necessary and there are indications that the god-parent relationship, i.e., kin by choice, came to have new meaning at this time.

A striking example of just such sponsorship is described by the wife of the American Ambassador in 1841. She had met George Hudson, the railway 'king', at a concert he gave in his palatial home and she says:

> These things are managed in a curious way here. A nouveau riche gets several ladies of fashion to patronise their entertainment and invite all the guests even if he has a wife. Lady Parke entertained for the Hudsons whose guest list included the Duke of Wellington. Lady Parke stood at the entrance of the splendid suite of rooms to receive the guests and introduce them to their host and hostess.[31]

Personal contacts channelled through Society also made nineteenth-century British politics extremely flexible with an interchange of

information and personnel across party lines ensuring continuity of
the governing group.

> My mother, strong Liberal as she was, had her reasons for
> maintaining her early friendship with Dizzy (Disraeli), and the
> results became apparent when she was able to bring her son-in-
> law Sir M. W. Ridley into personal contact with him, thus lead-
> ing to his first political appointment as Under-Home Secretary.[32]

As time went on, entertainments which had begun as private house
party events were opened to a somewhat wider elite.[33] These included
such occasions as the preview of the Royal Academy which was by
private invitation before the general attendance. All these extra,
semi-sporting rural or artistic events which were included in the
official Season were within easy reach of London. The mornings during the Season were riding in Rotten Row, to see and to be seen
balanced by driving in the park in the later afternoon for much the
same purpose. A pre-season in April was added later and a mini-
season in Brighton just after Christmas for those who didn't go
abroad. Yachting at Cowes in August which had also developed from
private beginnings, as the programme of the Royal Yacht Squadron,
was timed to coincide with the Queen's residence at Osborne, and
ended the official London-centred series of events.

There followed the August twelfth pilgrimage north for grouse
shooting. But country life, no matter how remote, did not necessarily
end political activity.

> The doors of Highland (i.e., Anglo-Scottish) houses always
> stood open and thus an informal and pleasant mode of intercourse
> sprang up which also had important results to the country, for
> when politicians of different parties were fellow guests under the
> same roof for a week or more, with many opportunities of talking
> over public questions as they rode or walked or made expeditions
> together, differences were apt to be smoothed over and com-
> promises effected.[34]

In the later autumn, country house parties gathered for partridge
shooting followed by hunting. Hunting was the activity *par excellence*
which brought together local people and those involved in London
Society. It had all the elements of aristocratic patronage and deference
masked by a male equality in sports. But the cost of maintaining the
horses and dogs, the beaters and coverts, meant that it also provided

an unsurpassed sphere of social aggrandisement for the new rich.[35] Hunting, too, allowed a limited amount of class mixing in the field: that is, local farmers, doctors and similar people could hunt along with the great as long as they were sufficiently keen and skilful. It is interesting to note, also, that hunting and riding were the only outlet for physical activity allowed even mid-Victorian girls and women. And when out in the field, the very strict rules of chaperonage had to be relaxed.[36]

The final or high point of the hunting season was the Hunt Ball. This was one of the more public functions of the social year in the sense that tickets were sometimes actually sold but many were also sent to private householders in return for a subscription. They were then allowed to make up their own private parties to attend and arrival with the correct set was important in visible social placing. The Ball took place usually

> In the Town Hall or best Inn . . . the arms of local nobility were displayed on the walls alongside portraits of aldermen and other notables. The company is composed partly of visitors and partly of natives, the visitors being mostly swells from London and other distant places and having the conventional manners and customs of such; but the natives may be distinguished by something more of an individual character, and there is just a tinge of the rural in their aspect.[37]

The London party usually entered later than local participants who tended to keep to their own end of the dance hall. But despite this spatial and temporal segregation of a fairly obvious kind, these occasions did seem to bring a certain cross current of sophistication to the smaller centres and a return to country roots to the cosmopolitans who took part.[38]

Until the end of the 1860s when it was still possible to have breakfast at country houses within walking distance of the city centre, for example in Hampstead, or to hunt in Finchley, these sports were a natural part of many establishments. Later came the division between essentially weekend houses in the country with large gardens, and great country establishments, now much more easily reached by train, where longer visits were paid. The special activity of the latter was sport whereas the former still played an important part in politics and the arts. Still later on, the growth of London-centred activities and the lengthening of the London Season meant that more remote

country seats might be neglected.[39] Mrs Gaskell in *Wives and
Daughters*, shows how local middle-class groups reacted to the frequent absences of the family 'at the Towers'. Indeed one of her
implied critical comparisons between this comparatively nouveau
arrivée family and the local squire is their following of the national
season to the neglect of local affairs. This may be a somewhat over-
simplified view, although one recent sociological study of a Scottish
border village confirms this picture of a gap between the 'cosmo-
politan' world of the aristocracy and local leadership of farmers, vicar
and schoolmaster in the history of the parish:

> The class of highest prestige was the 'county' owners of large
> tracts of land and persons with hereditary titles and their near
> relatives. One such family owned most of the farms in the
> parish.

They did not, however, farm any of it themselves or maintain a
household near the village:

> In many respects the county was utterly different in culture
> from the other classes. Whether as scholars and patrons of the
> arts or as devotees of the pleasures of hunting and opulent
> hospitality they moved in realms the others might admire but
> not enter.[40]

In Ireland and Wales, of course, language and religion as well as
culture divided this nationwide group from their indigenous localities.
In this situation, the professionals such as lawyers, land-agents,
doctors, ministers (and their wives) could act as go-betweens or take
on leadership activities in their own right.[41] But more local studies are
needed. In the absence of such studies, we just do not know what was
the effect of the absence or presence of wealthy and elite families on
local politics, the local economy or the local poor as well as on local
Society.

As public school and University education became a more important part of upper-class life, their annual high points, at Eton,
Henley or Lords, were amalgamated with other sporting and
artistic events. By the 1870s the calendar of social events for a
national Society with its blend of rural and urban pursuits was almost
complete. Its imperative demand for conformity for those who
accepted its rulings was such that some who could not afford the continual shuttle between London and the country were rumoured to have

closed the shutters of their London house and lived a secret troglodyte existence in the back rooms throughout August and September until it was decent to be seen in Town again.[42] Did this ever actually happen? It is impossible to know for certain. The circulation of such rumours itself is a sign of the power of 'Society' dictates.

This Society of the 1850s to 1870s was still small enough to be dominated by known individual personalities. In structure it resembled a vast pyramid of interlocking spiders' webs. At each level the individuals within the web had a sense of community as deep as any of Bethnal Green's[43] although the relatives, friends and neighbours might be scattered from County Cork to Essex, Sutherland to Dorset.

The building of this sense of community started early in childhood. For example, Hamilton Gardens, which was a section of Hyde Park enclosed by iron railings and a locked gate to which only select residents of Mayfair had keys, was used as a private playground for upper-class children. During the week in the Season, Nannies overlooked the children of the aristocracy playing together with the offspring of those professional men, bankers and other gentlemen whose wealth and family ties gave them admittance to these circles. This pattern of private communal gardens was imitated on a lesser scale all over the West End. Beyond, in Rotten Row:

> for an hour or two before luncheon and dinner its aspect was that of a garden party, for which, indeed, no invitations were necessary, but on which as a fact few persons intruded who would have been visibly out of place on the lawn of Marlborough House.[44]

This semi-private character of London's West End, resembling the layout of a gigantic country house, is sketched with bitterly clever sarcasm by H. G. Wells in *Tono Bungay*.

> 'By Jove!' said I, 'but this is the little assemblage of cases of stuffed birds and animals upon the Bladesover staircase grown enormous, and yonder as the corresponding thing to the Bladesover curios and porcelain is the Art Museum, and there in the observatories in Exhibition Road is old Sir Cuthbert's Gregorian telescope that I hunted out in the storeroom and put together.'[45]

The display function of these events should not be overlooked.

Although access to them was tightly controlled and the politically vital centres were private, many of the events could be viewed by members of the public. At Ascot, Henley, the Derby and similar sporting events, the insiders, sometimes literally behind bars as in the Royal Enclosure at Ascot, could be viewed by the public, middle- as well as working-class. The pageant of splendour impressed the populace while whetting the appetite of the ambitious.

Before the First World War, Drawing Rooms were held at 3 p.m. in the afternoon when the full glory of the upper classes could be seen wending its way towards Buckingham Palace.

In the Victorian reign, the superbly-gowned women, wearing magnificent tiaras and shining with jewels, sitting waiting their turn in St. James Park in state coaches that were brought out only on these full-dress occasions, were a joy to behold. The bewigged coachmen, sitting in solitary glory on the resplendent hammercloths, and the powdered footmen in liveries heavy with silver or gold, standing on ledges at the back of these historic carriages, clinging to the embroidered straps, were also part of the show. The entrance court of the Palace, with the guard of honour of Household Cavalry and its braying band and the beefeaters in their quaint Elizabethan costumes . . .[46]

One other important location of acceptable social interaction was the private home allotted to the head of official institutions. Official entertaining had always played an important part in the consolidation of the elite. It became even more crucial in the nineteenth century. In the armed services, universities, the higher levels of the church and in the diplomatic corps, the wife of the highest ranking official automatically became a hostess at the Bishop's Palace, Government House, the Master's Lodge (after dons were permitted to marry) or the headmaster's residence. Her skill as hostess was recognised as being essential to her husband's career just as much as for the woman who had 'married a country house'. The Season followed by these official hostesses differed slightly from the standard although many also took part in London Society. The high points in the church calendar, the university year, special visits from foreign dignitaries were all celebrated with various types of entertainment. Social difficulties began to arise over appointments to such positions when merit rather than breeding or wealth became a more important criterion of office holding.[47]

1. Park Lane, 1895, one of the principal thoroughfares of Society.

2. Tea in the West End. Little knots of footmen and pages waiting for their mistresses outside the confectioners' shops in Regent Street was a common sight.

OF THE WORLD WORLDLY.

"THERE GO THE SPICER WILCOXES, MAMMA! I'M TOLD THEY'RE DYING TO KNOW US. HADN'T WE BETTER CALL!"
"CERTAINLY NOT, DEAR. IF THEY'RE DYING TO KNOW US, THEY'RE NOT WORTH KNOWING. THE ONLY PEOPLE WORTH *OUR* KNOWING ARE THE PEOPLE WHO *DON'T* WANT TO KNOW US!"

3. (*left*) The 'cut'. The walk in Hyde Park could be an unnerving experience.

4. (*bottom left*) The United Services Club, 1883.

5. (*right*) A Court beauty in Presentation clothes, 1906.

6. (*below*) Instruction in Presentation etiquette at Fiffirella's, the gown shop, 1923.

7. (*top left*) The Empire
Promenade, 1902. The theatre
became one of the public
occasions for Society to meet.

8. (*right*) Presentation at Court,
1891. The pinnacle of the Season
for every debutante.

9. (*top right*) The Royal
Academy Exhibition, a standard
fixture in the circuit of the
Season.

THE AMBITIOUS MOTHER AND THE OBLIGING CLERGYMAN.

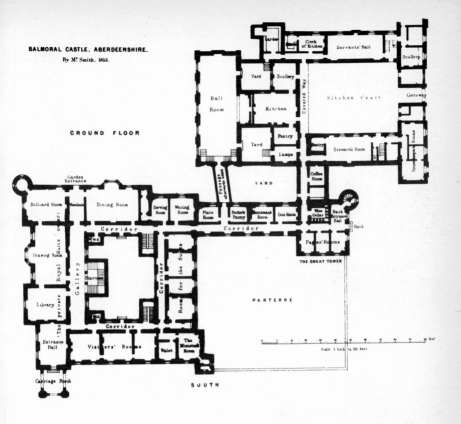

BALMORAL CASTLE, ABERDEENSHIRE.

By Mr Smith, 1855.

GROUND FLOOR

Garden
Entrance

Billiard Room   Vestibule   Dining Room   Serving Room   Waiting Room   Plate Room   Butler's Pantry   Steward's Room   Gun Room   Wine Cellar   Back Entrance Hall

Drawing Room   (The Royal Suite over)   Gallery (The private

Corridor   Corridor

Staircase   Corridor   Room for the Suite

Library

Corridor

Entrance Hall

Visitors' Rooms   Valet   The Minister's Room

Carriage Porch

SOUTH

Garden   Clerk of Kitchen   Servants' Hall   Scullery

Yard   Scullery

Ball Room   Kitchen   Covered Way   Kitchen Court   Gateway

Pantry

Yard   Lamps   Pantry   Stewards Room   Housekeeper's Room

YARD

Coffee Room

Passage (servants)

Pages' Rooms

THE GREAT TOWER

PARTERRE

Back

Scale 1 Inch to 30 Feet

10. (*top left*) The wedding, for so many mothers the height of ambition for their daughters.

11. (*bottom left*) A house party at Balmoral, 1865.

12. (*above*) The ground plan of Balmoral Castle showing the logistics of Society entertaining.

13. Dinner in Anglo-Indian Society.

14. The Anglo-Indian version of the hunt.

The domesticating of public life via the dictates of Society was combined with control of individual behaviour and face-to-face interaction through a rigidly applied code of personal behaviour. The increase in wealth for the middle and upper classes was being matched by an increase in the expected standard of living as the luxuries of one generation became the necessities of the next.[48] The personal reactions to the anomic situation produced by continually increasing material wealth are described in a classical passage by Durkheim. He has made the point that in the case of economic disaster something like a 'declassification' occurs. He goes on to say:

It is the same if the source of the crisis is an abrupt growth of power and wealth. Then truly, as the conditions of life are changed, the standard according to which needs were regulated can no longer remain the same; for it varies with social resources, since it largely determines the share of each class of producers. The scale is upset; but a new scale cannot be immediately improvised. Time is required for the public conscience to reclassify men and things. So long as the social forces thus freed have not regained equilibrium, their respective values are unknown and so all regulation is lacking for a time. The limits are unknown between the possible and the impossible, what is just and what is unjust, legitimate claims and hopes and those which are immoderate. Consequently there is no restraint upon aspirations.[49]

He goes on to postulate a connection between 'anomic' suicide and such crises. But there are other social and psychological reactions to such a situation than the extreme of self-destruction. This is not to argue that there was a mechanistic reaction to sudden wealth and possibilities of unlimited consumption. Rather, it should be a case of looking to see which groups took part in the change in domestic behaviour; for example, which individual families stopped drinking so heavily or started regular church-going. Keeping in mind these general qualifications it is still possible to recognise certain features of the religious revival in the early nineteenth century as part of an attempt at control over personal behaviour just as was the emphasis put on the home as the seat of moral goodness. Personal sobriety, cleanliness, orderliness and punctuality went together with both of these trends. The strict segregation by age, by sex and by social category which began to be enforced in public institutions as well as in the family can also be seen as a reaction against the growing chaos in

3

social relationships at a time of unprecedented population growth and social change.[50]

The fact is sometimes overlooked that the upper and middle classes as well as the working class participated in the rise in population. Indeed, with their higher expectation of life it was they who had the best chance of raising their large families to maturity. Families with large numbers of surviving children growing up in the midst of challenging new social conditions could present real problems of control to the older generations.[51] It may be that the strict emphasis on filial duty, especially for girls,[52] and the formality of home life for the middle classes which began in pre-Victorian England were responses to these new conditions. Those born into the aristocracy and sure of their birthright might continue to flout the new stricter morality but unless their manners and behaviour were such as to be tolerated in a fair number of drawing-rooms, there was a danger that they would be absent from important decision-making centres, not least the new Court under Victoria. Middle-class governesses and tutors in aristocratic families were sometimes expected to enforce these codes on the new generation. In turn the younger generation tried to reform their elders' morals and conduct almost in the spirit of the Young Pioneers. Such struggles are well illustrated in the early-nineteenth-century Duchess of Devonshire's ménage where Sara Trimmer was governess.[53]

In the middle class, whose resources were more limited, one of the most effective forces of control over their children, their dependants and themselves was the strict ordering of time; diurnal, weekly and seasonal. Only monastic and religious orders had ever controlled behaviour through the day with such minute exactitude as the Victorians. The introduction of strict timekeeping, indeed the use of accurate clocks and later individual watches, had been a gradual and slow process, connected with commercial and mercantile occupations. But in the nineteenth century it became the way of life for virtually all the middle and upper class. In the eighteenth century the introduction of regular schedules for coaches had made some fixed timekeeping necessary for those who travelled frequently. But the aim of the prosperous middle class and particularly the upper class had been to have their own long-distance transport; an entire private coach with postillion if possible but at least a private carriage. It was the introduction of train travel at fixed times and fixed destinations that did so much to create boundaries of time units in people's minds. The great nobleman might force the station master to make the train wait on his pleasure but there were very few who could successfully challenge the schedules of the railways.

As the agricultural calendar of feasts and fairs, the rural workday of dawn till dusk, lost their saliency, it became possible to allot special times to social and other activities in a more arbitrary way. Meal times, work times, dressing times, visiting times were at exact intervals and breaches of timekeeping were treated as much a moral lapse as a breach of good taste.[54] It is not accidental that the early nineteenth century was the period when gongs and house bells were introduced on a wide scale.[55]

The custom of holding family prayers for the whole household spread gradually from the 1830s until it was a practice widespread throughout the upper and middle class. This custom united all the elements of control so far discussed into one of the most significant rituals of Victorian life. All segregated categories of the household, e.g., servants, children, adults and visitors, were gathered together at the same hour every day punctually summoned by the ringing of a bell or gong before the adult breakfast was served. This was the only time that all met together so that the occasion reinforced the idea of community, an organic whole made up of functionally separate parts. The segregation was maintained in the seating arrangements with adult family at the front, children next, servants behind 'and the governess worshipping a little apart' (Thackeray). Family prayers were almost invariably held in the dining-room or hall, almost never in the drawing-room which was preserved for ceremonial social activities. Thus a public act of worship was brought into the most private sanctum of the household, i.e., where meals were eaten together. Private family worship, believed to be a prime duty placed on the Master/Father of this small hierachical kingdom, was seen as one of the keystones of the social fabric and as having an immediate impact on the lower members of the household.

By the turn of the century there was a growing realisation that worship in such a secular setting was incongruous. Remaining in the proper frame of mind while kneeling on the carpet, pressing one's face against the dining-room horsehair (some children thought of family prayers as 'smelling the chairs'), when the only view was rows of maids' stiff apron bows, when the smell of bacon and coffee assailed one's nose and impatient rings at the front door distracted even the master himself, was too much for most of the younger generation and slowly the custom was shifted to once a week on Sunday evenings, and, as leisure activities for all age groups grew more varied, was finally abandoned.

The unique feature of Victorian society is that these essentially middle-class patterns of behaviour were grafted on to the honorific code of the aristocracy or gentry to produce the widened concept of 'gentility', which was, without doubt, one of the most effective instruments for social control ever devised. This was achieved by the middle class permeating the ranks of the aristocracy, particularly the gentry, either literally in person or by the spread of its values. This amalgamation did not occur without a struggle. For example, at the beginning of the century an important issue was the opposition to duelling, not because of the violence involved but because it represented part of the traditional code of honour. This code emphasised valour, physical courage, romantic attributes of heritage and ran counter to the values of personal effort, work and achievement.[56]

As the century wore on, very slowly the calendar of events in the pursuit of gentlemanly life, sport, social intercourse, entertainment and dining, was formalised, enlarged and organised into separate activities, pursued at specific times. Personal behaviour was also modified and controlled. Very slowly the business of pleasure and government took on the habits—and hours—of business.[57]

CHAPTER III

· ❋ ·

The Anatomy of Society and Etiquette

Society, at whatever level one cares to look at it, is not easy to define. As Virginia Woolf said in *Orlando*, 'London Society is a miasma—a mirage . . . At one and the same time Society is everything and Society is nothing. Society is the most powerful concoction in the world and Society has no existence whatsoever' . . .[1] In sociological terms Society is a self-defined status group based on communal lifestyles. The ever-changing rules of fashion often become an element in control by such groups although, as Weber rightly emphasises, lifestyles and fashions are almost invariably supported by the ownership of some sort of property.[2] Such groups, through social interaction (Weber's connubium and commensality) often bar aspiring others from the acquisition of privileged economic and political positions, for one of the most important privileges of being in Society is having access to a vast information network: information about jobs, investment possibilities, secret political decisions. At the *same time* participation in the group is a reward and a badge of arrival into these positions, a public seal of acceptance into elite status.

A feature of this kind of social group is that entry, by either an individual or family, is voluntary. An eccentric could choose to define himself as not 'being in Society' although he had all the requisite requirements for being accepted. Even the most eligible through birth, wealth and education might choose to live as a recluse and care nothing for the reactions of relatives or the public. A notorious example was the Duke of Bedford who kept two large fully staffed houses in London complete with four cars and eight chauffeurs as well as the army of 50–60 servants at Woburn, yet he lived virtually cut off from social, political or even family life.[3]

Nor did everyone who made money quickly in the various boom

periods during the century choose to enter Society. They might
rather put energy and capital back into the family enterprise. Some
chose family or church ties alone. The immediate descendants of such
families may have felt themselves a little outside the upper-class
machinery for entering fully into national Society, yet too wealthy and
important for local Society. Whatever the cause, the decision to remain strictly within the family circle or socially isolated had direct
effects on the lives of all in the household but particularly the girls
and unmarried daughters. Beatrix Potter, who was educated at home,
as so many girls of her class, never made the transition 'into Society'
and therefore never had any opportunity to break from the complete
submission to her parents authority. Not a single institution even of a
semi-public kind was open to her to contest this authority.[4]

Among the lower middle class (George Grossmith's 'Pooters') the
attempt to enter Society at even a very modest level often required too
great an effort. For young couples starting their married life there
are many warnings in magazines and advice books not to try to go
into Society at first, or at least at not too high a level.[5] These warnings tended to be directed at urban and suburban audiences where a
certain material level was necessary as a base. On the other hand in
more closed villages or small towns confidence and presence could
bring off what was, in many cases, a self-fulfilling definition of
acceptability. Louisa Potter, who wrote about the mid-Victorian
provincial scene with acute insight says:

> I wonder what constitutes gentility! . . . I believe in assuming
> to yourself and others that you are genteel; and only assume it
> enough, and all around you will come into the belief. In every
> country neighbourhood there is a genteel family, it may be poor
> —that is of no consequence; if it thinks itself genteel, the neigh-
> bours think so too.[6]

But, although there was an element of choice involved, most families
realised that in order to gain access to positions of power or to consolidate gains already made, it was necessary to enter Society at some
level while realising that to be recognised at the desired level it
might be necessary to wait until one's children were properly
groomed in the appropriate life-style before full acceptance was
granted.[7]

The traditional aristocracy, both nobility and gentry, had had little
need to seek a legitimating ideology for their continued rule. But such

certainty, shaken by the events of the 1830s and 1840s, needed a more explicit framework, especially in the case of the relative new-comers to wealth and power. The justification for their way of life, partially derived from the renewed emphasis on a Christian ethic, was in terms of a vague but complex idea of 'social duty': duty to them-selves, their families, their social strata and the community as a whole. One strand in this ideal derived from simple economic ideas about the benefits of middle-class consumption in providing work for other classes.[8] But beyond this, it was the duty of the middle- and upper-class family to maintain an establishment on the most elaborate scale they could afford, in order to entertain and interact in a civilised way, as an example to the barbarous customs of their native lower class and natives overseas. The feeling was:

> That the responsibilities of Society are very great and can in no way be evaded is true for no one denies that the vices of Society have a disastrous effect on the nation at large.[9]

Whether or not this was true, even in more remote country districts, is a very debatable question. It is the belief in their own importance which justified their behaviour to themselves. This concept con-tinued to be used to justify what could be looked at as an intensely selfish way of life based on leisure, sport, dining and entertainment, long after its country estate context had faded away.

Such ideals of social duty and the legitimate supremacy of Society activities were, by definition, conservative. It is true that many new-comers were absorbed into elite positions through Society while impecunious members of the elite were gently lowered into respect-able poverty, but this mobility took place within an extremely hier-archical, even rigidly formal social structure. Those who ignored the system, or even worse, those who took a stand against it, were seen as potentially hostile, threatening and disruptive. The sanctions which could be invoked by Society in terms of ostracism, ridicule and exclusion from sources of power and wealth were extremely powerful.

As British control over the Empire grew, so did the feeling that the British upper and middle class was the centre of the social world. The opulence and extravagance of these groups was justified by invoking the idea of social duty. But the lavish expenditure of time, energy and money sometimes weighed heavily on the individual conscience, for the ideals of duty were based on Christian precepts of individual conduct and behaviour. For many, and especially many women, an

even stricter adherence to personal and individual standards of behaviour within their own circle in an effort to still that conscience only
made it more difficult to develop an understanding of wider social
problems in general or a genuine sympathy with the problems of
working-class life in particular.[10] It was felt that in some way their
own personal behaviour would stand as examples to the working
class even in the minutiae of living. Thus card playing on Sundays
should be banned as it set a bad example to the servants. And, when
speaking of setting an example to the lower classes, most women
really meant their servants who were the only representatives of
another class they saw at close quarters and whose deferential
response, outwardly at least, reinforced the seeming importance of
formal propriety and individual gentility.

Such an inherent blindness was particularly acute for women who
were cut off from the correctives of involvement with wider political
or economic life, and at least among middle-class families, social
duties were interpreted as more imperative for women than for men.
Indeed, in a legal hand book it is stated that a wife was legally bound
to live up to her husband's position in Society no matter what her own
inclinations or family responsibilities might be.[11] This does not mean
that men did not accept their social duty to marry and establish a
family, to entertain and be received in an appropriate social sphere.
On the contrary, they were very much aware of the advantages for
furthering their interests and broadcasting their successes which playing a part in Society alone could bestow. The problem, as Banks has so
convincingly demonstrated, was how to finance and maintain the
establishment which such a position demanded. Conventional
marriage implied providing an income and managing such an establishment plus the added burden of unlimited numbers of children. And
conventional marriage was the only legitimate way of establishing a
permanent relationship with a woman. It is possible to speculate that
one of the consequences of this pattern, which made such heavy
demands on middle- and upper-class men, was not only to postpone
marriage but also to push many of them into homosexual relationships
as well as relationships with working-class girls.[12] Speculation apart,
in the early part of the period when the 'pay-off' from Society functions
was greater, 'even for men of conspicuous talent, Society was a
matter as serious as politics or any war'.[13] Even then, it was women
who carried on many of the day-to-day social activities.

INTRODUCTIONS, CALLS AND DINING

The means by which each level of society created barriers to entry was the elaborate code of etiquette which grew up from the 1820s onwards. (The word etiquette significantly means labelling or ticketing.) The most ceremonial behaviour was required for those times in the life cycle which have, in all cultures, been used to mark 'rites de passage' . . . birth, coming of age, marriage and death. The other sensitive area ruled by etiquette was the introduction of new individuals and families into group membership and activities. The introductions, calls, various levels of 'commensality' and their obverse—the 'cut'—became vastly elaborated.[14]

In a system where the aim was to keep those below you at bay while gaining access to the next higher group, introductions were vitally important: 'ladies will pay a very special attention to this important rite'. The inferior was always introduced to the superior, who ideally should have been asked beforehand if he or she wished to be introduced. The higher in rank, the older and the woman (among women, the married) were those to whom the newcomer was introduced. If there was any question about supremacy, rank always took precedence. The socially more important then had the choice of following up the introduction or not by further recognition. (It should be noted that it was only in England that women acknowledged introductions which shows, perhaps, their very real social power.)

Being introduced then, was only the first step. A mid-century manual aimed at the newly arrived provincial warns:

> It is neither necessary nor desirable to introduce everybody to everybody; and the promiscuous presentations sometimes inflicted upon us are anything but agreeable. You confer no favour on us, and only a nominal one to the person presented, by making us acquainted with one whom we do not desire to know; and you may inflict a positive injury upon both. You also put yourself in an unpleasant position; for 'an introduction *is a social endorsement*', and you become, to a certain extent, responsible for the person you introduce. If he disgraces himself in any way you share, in a greater or lesser degree, in his disgrace. Be as cautious in this matter as you would in writing your name on the back of another man's note.[15]

The separation of initial introduction and real acceptance is indicated by the existence of 'the English rule' (so called by Americans)[16] i.e. 'the roof is an introduction'. Once invited to the home no further sign of social acceptability such as an introduction was considered necessary.[17]

If the higher status party did not want to continue the relationship they 'cut'. This was used extensively, not to humiliate in a personal way, but by devices such as on meeting in public crossing the street or not catching the eye or at most a 'cold civil salute'. This practice led to the idiomatic use of 'know'. 'Do you know Mr X?' 'No, I have met him, but I don't know (i.e. recognise) him.' This is a phrase frequently used in Victorian dialogue and should be recognised as a consequence of Society rules. Non-participants like servants could not introduce or cut. Nor, it is interesting to note, could functionaries like clergymen, doctors or governesses.

In general the next step in social recognition after being introduced, was the leaving of cards (although sometimes the higher rank could leave cards on the lower without being introduced as a special favour). In the eighteenth century the custom had been at large town houses to have a slate where callers' names were written. In the country callers were most often neighbours, house guests or relatives. But by about 1800 the French custom of using printed cards to leave in place of personal visits became widespread. The leaving of cards added an intermediate step in the interaction between the parties which made the system more flexible and at the same time less damaging personally. Ideally a lady seated in her carriage handed her card to her servant who took it to the door and handed it to the servant of the house who took it to his mistress who could then decide whether or not she was 'At Home' to the caller. Sending cards in advance of a subsequent call also put a time interval between the contact of the parties. Seen in this way, 'the stress laid by Society upon the correct usage of these magic bits of paste-board, will not seem unnecessary, when it is remembered that the visiting card, socially defined means, and frequently is, made to take the place of one's self.'[18]

By mid-century it was acknowledged that the wife could deputise for her husband by leaving his card, while grown-up daughters accompanying their mothers had their names printed underneath. A lady left her own card and two of her husband's, one for the lady of the house and one for the master. If the corner of the card was turned down it meant that the card had been delivered in person, with the intention of calling, not by a servant.

The importance of the initial contact through cards is shown in a recalled incident where a newcomer left cards on the writer's mother who had had no intentions of calling on her as she was a social inferior. The mother wrote a stiff letter pointing out that initiating a call in this way was not in the social code. Mrs X, the newcomer, found out that her schoolboy son had, as a joke, taken some cards from the silver salver in someone else's hall. (Where they were always left displayed to let other callers see who had left cards.) Mrs X. made many apologies for this inadvertent faux-pas but was never called on by the writer's mother until both families lost sons in the First World War when the social barriers were, at last, lowered.[19]

Card leaving, however, was not synonymous with calling. It was, rather, a system of feeling the social climate before taking action. A leader entitled 'Etiquette' says:

> There is very strict etiquette in this matter of cards and calls and there is one essential difference between *calling* and *leaving cards*. It is usual on paying a first visit merely to leave cards without inquiring if the mistress of the house is at home. Thus Mrs. A. leaves her own card and two of her husband's cards upon Mrs. B. Within a week, if possible, certainly within ten days Mrs. B. should return the visit and leave cards upon Mrs. A. Should Mrs. A., however, have 'called' upon Mrs. B. and the latter returned it by merely leaving cards this would be taken as a sign that the latter did not desire the acquaintance to ripen into friendship. Strict etiquette demands that a call should be returned by a call and a card by a card.[20]

Calls were also made on ceremonial occasions, e.g. after marriage, or childbirth. They were also used as acknowledgement of hospitality received, always within three days of dining or attending a ball, reception or other entertainment. These calls between acquaintances were confined to the middle of the afternoon so as not to disrupt the housekeeping and business side of the household. They were termed 'morning calls'. The official timetable for visiting was 3 p.m. to 4 p.m. for ceremonial calls, 4 p.m. to 5 p.m. for semi-ceremonial calls and 5 p.m. to 6 p.m. for intimate calls. Sunday was traditionally a day for closer friends and family. These were somewhat revised later in the century when there was a much heavier social calendar, and popular and active people regularly attended two or even three houses in an evening, a practice called 'dining deep'.

Manuals of etiquette stressed that calls should be short and formal with conversation restricted to light, pleasant and impersonal topics. No children or dogs, or other intrusive extras should be taken. In paying morning calls, it was correct to keep on outdoor clothing, men particularly had to keep hat, gloves, walking stick in order to emphasise the ritual nature of the call. Fifteen minutes was considered long enough for this purpose. If several people called simultaneously including relatives, then the strict procedure of introductions was brought into play. It was in the course of calling that wives made the contacts which led to dinner invitations which in turn might mean entry into important houses and during the course of afternoon calls, the women of the family could collect useful information about the social network. Conversely for those few who wanted to stay out of the social game it was possible to call a halt in the proceedings without giving offence. A couple in the 1890s who were both writers wanting time to work at their profession migrated to Eastbourne but never felt part of the social life there. The wife told her daughter that, to preserve their isolation, she returned all calls but refused the first invitation to tea and gave no invitations herself. [21]

Young and unmarried men paid their calls on Sundays, a practice sometimes called, a little maliciously, 'sowing seeds'. On the whole, however, they were rather pitied for having to do so as it was considered very much a part of a wife's or daughter's duty. In the later part of the period when other activities for sport, travel and voluntary work were opened to women, paying calls was increasingly regarded as being something of a burden. In defending the practice, the writers on etiquette reveal even more clearly how important the system was in maintaining the fabric of Victorian hierarchy.

Visits of form of which most people complain and yet to which most people submit, are absolutely necessary—being in fact, the basis on which that great structure, society mainly rests. You cannot invite people to your house, however often you may have met them elsewhere, until you have first called upon them in a formal manner, and they have returned the visit. It is a kind of safeguard against any acquaintances which are thought to be undesirable. If you do not wish to continue the friendship, you discontinue to call, and that is considered an intimation of such intentions, and therefore no further advances are made by them. But it would be considered very bad manners, and very un-courteous behaviour, not to return a call in the first instance.[22]

Cards were also left to show that the family were leaving the area for a while (with P.P.C. written on them—Pour Prend Congé). Frequently absences could be used to change an individual's or family's social milieu, sometimes radically, for instance, by going abroad. On returning from such an absence, the choice of *whom* to call on could be used to form a new social set. Among an elite that was constantly shifting from town to country this was extremely important. Indeed, the whole elaborate structure was most useful in cities where face-to-face interaction is always harder to maintain. There was, for example, the growing problem of the 'placing' of town dwellers who temporarily rented a place in the country as opposed to the landed family (or at least country dwelling family) who rented a house in the town for the Season. In the country, the parties may have been acquainted and on calling terms. Back in town 'the Park divides them' (Hyde Park).[23]

The technique of card leaving and calling continued to be used as more people wished to live in more distant suburbs. A common pattern was to rent a country house for a short time in an area where eventually the family would decide to live permanently as commuters. Then the preliminary social step between residents (often poorer gentry) and newcomers was the exchange of calls:

> The resident is the first to take the initiative. If it is adverse to the result desired for instance, if one feels she is not likely to care much about knowing the other from what is gathered in the course of a quarter of an hour's conversation, the acquaintance comes to a deadlock, whichever side may feel disinclined to continue it, as it cannot be a one-sided one and maintained by one of the two only.[24]

Although the system of etiquette was highly formalised, its details were constantly changing. These subtle shifts of fashionably correct behaviour were used to mark the knowledgeable insider from the outsider. As Society rules became more complex and greater numbers of people were involved, magazines began to act as advice centres on questions of social behaviour.[25] Starting in the 1880s *The Queen* ran a regular etiquette column, 'Au Fait'. Unfortunately only the answers

were published so that it is only possible to guess at the readers'
problems. For example, in November 1894, 'Nemo' is answered:

> She should not have bowed to either his wife or himself. They
> probably thought they had met her somewhere but were not
> quite sure. Casual conversation at an afternoon party does not
> establish a bowing acquaintance—the correct way is to affect
> not to have seen them.

There is nothing which so divided the life-styles of the middle class
and working class as the formality of calling and visiting. Any middle
class or upper class person felt free to visit a working class home at
any time, to walk in and at once become involved in the life of the
family by asking questions, dispensing charity or giving orders. This
might be tempered by personal kindness and considerateness, especially on estates and in villages in the country, but the fact remains
that there was an unquestioned *right* to act in this way.

An ex-cook who had married the gamekeeper and lived in the
Lodge described, without resentment, the effects of such an expectation. She always felt that she had to 'keep baby nice because you never
knew who they (the Gentry) were bringing in'. A frequent guest at
the Hall, when out walking the dog in the estate grounds, would call
in, 'didn't matter what time of day it was, she'd go and fetch baby out
of her cot. And she'd say, I'm never afraid to fetch her out of her cot
because she's kept as well as if she was in my own nursery. I did hear
her say that to this Lady and I thought, oh well, that's a feather.'[26]

I have argued that the rituals of introductions, cards and calling
were in part established to give the parties time to accept or reject
social interaction. In contrast, working-class servants and other functionaries were expected to be instantly available at any time they were
wanted by upper-class individuals. Servants were to be on call at any
hour, tradesmen to deliver goods at any time, anywhere. This expectation had very immediate consequences in the luxury trades. For
example, one of the greatest problems for dressmakers, milliners and
others in these occupations was the unevenness of demand. Hectic
overwork during the Season alternated with slack time out of it as
well as the rushing of orders for capricious customers who changed
their minds at the last minute.[27]

If introductions, calls and card leaving were 'the small change of
society, then balls and dinners are its heavy drafts' according to a
commercially-minded mid-Victorian.[28] Invitations to dinner were

often given according to the same precedence as introductions, and they were formally written at least two weeks in advance. The proper selection of dinner guests called for the highest application of social skills while bringing the greatest opportunity for social success or failure.

In the eighteenth century dining was more often than not an afternoon prelude to an evening at the theatre or public gardens. But in the nineteenth century, with the decline of public places of amusement for respectable families, dinner became the apogee of the social day.[29] The hour of dining was steadily put forward from about 2 p.m. to evening. In part this was to enable those men who had to work to finish their tasks. It was made possible by the introduction of better artificial lighting—first oil and then gas. Whatever the cause, it meant a change into more formal clothes and the introduction of new rituals. Precedence in the procession from the drawing-room, with the guests paired off male and female, marked conclusively the social rank of each participant. Their seating at the table set the seal on that rank. Handbooks for footmen and butlers contain tables of precedence and a very sharp eye was used to note mistakes. For example, to help the many newcomers to society, Burke published a *Book of Precedence* in 1881. It had an alphabetical list with a key number by each entry which 'indicates at a glance the positions of the various grades'. Burke maintained that the law of precedences, when strictly adhered to, 'regulates to general satisfaction everyone's proper position in society'. But the necessity for such a book indicates an uncertainty about social ranking at this period.[30]

Protocol of precedence had to be maintained within each hierarchical institution and difficulties could arise when position within these hierarchies cut across aristocratic definitions of place. It was the duty of the host (or more often the hostess) to smooth out all these problems. Raverat says of the 1890s:

> The regular round of formal dinner parties was very important in Cambridge. In our house the parties were generally of twelve or fourteen people, and everybody of dinner party status was invited strictly in turn. The guests were seated according to the Protocol, the Heads of Houses ranking by the dates of the foundations of their colleges, except that the Vice-Chancellor would come first of all. After the Masters came the Regius Professors in the order of their subjects, Divinity first; and then the

other Professors according to the dates of the foundations of their chairs, and so on down all the steps of the hierarchy.[31]

These gradations were supremely important to the participants and even at the very highest level it was not unknown for ladies to jockey for position, to the point of using elbows to advance their claim, as the Countess of Airlie discovered when she was Lady of the Bedchamber to Queen Mary. It was part of her duty to line up the ladies for dinner in strict order of precedence when 'there was always an argument as Winifred, Duchess of Portland, insisted on putting herself at the head, although the Duchess of Roxburgh was actually entitled to this place'.[32]

Within the family, too, precedence and related rituals could mark relative positions. For example, when, around 1900, Kathleen Smith, daughter of a wealthy merchant, was visiting her fiancé's home (he was a younger son of minor gentry) on the last evening of her visit she reported to her mother that she 'went in with him [the fiancé, Frank Isherwood] as it was the last night'. Christopher Isherwood, her son, points out the significance of this gesture. According to protocol Kathleen would naturally have 'gone in with' her father-in-law and Frank would have 'taken in' his mother. The changes of partner on the last evening was a 'sort of betrothal ceremony'.[33]

More elaborate service at dinner was one of the new fashions designed to display the greater use of the establishment's skilled man-power resources as well as to free the host and hostess for purely social functions. Before that time, the host carved at the table and two huge courses, each with a great variety of dishes, were put on the table one after the other. The new system of dinner 'à la Russe', first observed in the 1820s, required the footmen to carve at a side table and serve the food to each guest in turn.[34] Guests no longer poured wine for each other but waited for footmen to do it for them. In discussing these changes in custom, it must be remembered that there could be a considerable time lag in their adoption in different social sets and in the provinces as opposed to the capital. John Izzard Pryor, prosperous Hertfordshire brewer, was impressed when he first dined à la Russe when invited to meet the American Ambassador at Knebworth in 1852.[35] Some memoirs report that early Victorian or even pre-Victorian habits were still practised by their grandparents at the end of the century.

Increased wealth and 'plant' also made it possible to give private balls and dances instead of subscription dances in public assembly rooms. This was considered desirable as part of the move to restrict socially and sexually mixed functions in public. One of the reasons that private gatherings were preferred was that the invitations could be individually scrutinised and undesirable entries eliminated. Even later in the century when public functions were again gaining in popularity, the custom was to have private dinners or house parties before the public ball. It was entry to these *private* affairs which was coveted.[36]

Later in the century, as more men began to work regular office hours, and take meals away from home, luncheon and especially tea became socially important. But they were essentially ladies' meals, supplements to morning calls. Some women set fixed days for such afternoon affairs by being At Home on a wider or narrower basis, on set days of the week. In this way, middle-class patterns of social behaviour, most significantly the 'feminisation' of social life, were adopted by almost all groups eligible to be in Society.

SOCIETY AND MARRIAGE

One of the most essential points of access to high status group membership is through marriage. This avenue of advancement took on new significance during our period. It often provided status legitimacy through one partner and new capital through the other. Throughout the nineteenth century arranged marriages were no longer acceptable so that individual choice had to be most carefully regulated to ensure exclusion of undesirable partners and maximum gain for both sides. Social exclusiveness ensured the former. The latter was achieved by the strenuous bargaining which took place after the marriage proposal and acceptance. The two fathers, or their legal representatives, then came to grips with the terms of the marriage settlement.

Under such a system it was vital that only potentially suitable young people should mix. To meet these ends, balls and dances became the particular place for a girl to be introduced into Society. The name and rank of the young men who signed her dance programme (a custom introduced in the 1850s,[37] except among the most aristocratic, supposedly so well known to each other that programmes were considered 'rather second circle') were an indication of her social position as well as beauty and personal attraction. Chaperones were necessary to overlook the social character of her dancing partners just as much

4

as her sexual behaviour. The rule that a girl must not dance more than three dances with one partner or sit out a dance with a young man was to ensure rigid control of this most delicate situation where new family alliances might be made through marriage. For these functions, the girls had their own trade secrets, obviously mostly concerned with dress and fashion. They also had their own trade language, e.g. a socially eligible young man was a 'parti' (from bon-parti) while his opposite was a 'detrimental'. A 'squash' was a function that young girls attended out of duty rather than for their own interest or amusement.

Under this regime, it is not surprising that by mid-century the rules of chaperonage were very strict. An unmarried woman under thirty could not go anywhere or be in a room even in her own house with an unrelated man unless accompanied by a married gentlewoman or a servant. As a note it should be added that an unmarried gentlewoman, no matter how old, could not chaperone; she was still nominally unattached to the system. Governesses, on the other hand, although they were expected to come from genteel backgrounds, were allowed to chaperone although it was not necessary to chaperone them. This was felt to be humiliating as it showed they had dropped out of the system and were no longer in the marriage stakes. On the other hand, in practical terms, it gave them more personal independence.

Marriage was considered not so much an alliance between the sexes as an important social definition; serious for a man but imperative for a girl. It was part of her social duty to enlarge her sphere of influence through marriage. In order to marry a girl must have achieved the status of an adult. To become an adult, she must have entered Society at some level. In Trollope's *Ayala's Angel*, two sisters left orphaned are handed over to the care of two uncles. One uncle lives an absolutely secluded life with his wife, the other wealthy uncle's family follows the seasonal round with great verve. It is accepted that the sister who goes to the retiring couple will never marry.

The only other possibility for wider action was to become mistress of a father's or brother's home. If it was on a grand scale such a position could be more attractive than marriage since it meant social power without submission to a husband's rules.

When a sister is at the head of her brother's house, she always takes the position of a married woman in the estimation of her friends; the mantle of his presence in the household completely envelopes her in its folds of conventionality. The two are invited together to dinners, to dances, to At Homes, to everything.[38]

A striking example of this was the case of the sister of Viscount Berehaven, 4th Earl of Bantry. When her brother suddenly married, she was 'dethroned' and she married the first English aristocrat who came along. He carried her off to Leicestershire where she remained virtually a prisoner in the gigantic mausoleum, Staunton Harold.[39]

A girl's whole life from babyhood was oriented to the part she had to play in this 'status theatre'.[40] Although marriage was her greatest chance for expanding her role it was not the end of the play by any means. It was the progression through sharply demarcated stages in the move from one status to the next which made her life so different from her brothers'.[41] It also made what education she received meaningless to her future life.[42] From the time the little girl entered the schoolroom at about the age of five until she 'came out' at seventeen or eighteen, there was nothing to mark her progress in the way of promotions, certificates or even in variation in dress. Later in the period, some girls were sent away to school especially during their middle teens, some even to the Continent. Some were given a few added responsibilities at home in connection with running the house or less often with the younger children. But for most, early adolescence was an awkward time, not just because of their own physical and psychological development but because they had no place socially. The only 'safe' contacts they could have outside the home were with a few selected other girls, clergymen, or in the context of small-scale charity work, particularly teaching in Sunday schools. It is possible that religious confirmation, which usually took place about the ages of thirteen to fifteen and was accompanied with a certain amount of familial ritual, helped to reconcile them to the system and fill in the gap while they waited to come out. It absorbed idealistic energy which might have been turned in a more disruptive direction. A conventional girl, born 1863, wrote:

> I fancy that I thought taking the sacrament might make it easier to "be good" though what "being good" actually was became increasingly difficult to understand, unless it just meant doing what those "set in authority" over you wished.[43]

At seventeen or eighteen she suddenly emerged from the schoolroom. Hair was put up, skirts down and she was groomed, often by special deportment masters, to be presented at Court or its local equivalent. The metaphor used again and again is a butterfly emerging from a chrysalis.[44]

The change in required behaviour was also radical for 'although the schoolroom girl might appear at luncheon when neighbours came over or there was a party in the house, woe betide her if she ventured to say more than "Yes" or "No" to remarks addressed to her—as for a joke of any sort it was unthinkable! From the opposite side of the table a gorgon-eye would be fixed upon her, plainly intimating that she was transgressing the proprieties and freezing her to silence. With her "coming out" the position was reversed. What previously had been called reprehensible was now a virtue. It was impressed upon her that as a member of Society it was her duty to contribute her mite to the general pool.'[45]

If they were fortunate in having hospitable relatives and friends, teenage girls often went the rounds visiting with them, making social 'dry runs' before their first Season. For those who were presented at Court, the occasion took on an almost mystical significance. Weeks were spent in training to gracefully climb in and out of a carriage, to walk up stairs, to curtsey and walk out of the room backwards while encumbered by the long trailing Court train, long white veils, the ostrich feather and tiara head dress. The choosing and fitting of this gown and all its trimmings was a time-consuming occupation. On the day itself, when she was finally dressed and ready, the girl was admired by the whole household circle of relatives and servants whose deferential approval added to her feeling of importance. The drive to the palace, the long wait in the ante-room surrounded by the protocol of magnificently dressed Court functionnaries impressed on her that she was truly a part of the great national community. When she was at last admitted to the inner sanctum, this was reinforced by the ceremony which decreed that 'if the débutant was the daughter of a Peer, the Queen leant forward and kissed her; if the young lady was the daughter of a commoner she kissed Her Majesty's hand'.[46] And so she emerged fully fledged into a new adult category.

Two or three Seasons were all the chance she had; after that, if she were not at least engaged she was, for the most part, written off as a failure. A proper débutante was expected to keep a 'Season's Album', a record of social success, which she 'had to fill with the signatures of fellow guests and adorn with photographs of houses visited, enlivening the pages with verses, sketches or witty remarks contributed by her more talented friends'.[47] If she married—and especially married well—she emerged with a totally new status. In the fluid social climate of that time such a change was an opportunity to recoup or reconsider social position. Immediately after the ceremony, says the author of the *Bride's Book*,[48] 'sending bridal favours shows what circles you will mix with after marriage'.

The young matron then began the important task of setting up the plant and making use of the contacts for the new family unit. If she moved in upper-middle-class and aristocratic circles she was again presented at Court by her *husband's* female relatives to set the seal on her new status. Or if his family—or her own—were not sufficiently well-connected a friendly sponsor might be found. Mrs Lily Langtry was presented during her second season in London by the Marchioness of Conyngham at the same time as the Marchioness presented her daughter. 'We had arranged it during one of my visits to their country house.' However, 'having an official position in the Queen's Household, Lady Conyngham had the privilege of the "entrée" (private entrance to the Palace) but this she could not, of course, extend to anyone outside her own family. Therefore my actual companion on that day was Lady Rowney.' Thus those who had entered 'Society' on the basis of beauty and personality or talent alone tried to secure the most respectable of sponsors.[49]

The next important step in the matron's career, the birth of her babies, was marked by ceremonial visits, of course, but such customs as the wearing of white flowers or wrapping white ribbons on the door knocker died out by mid-century. Contrary to much of the moralising literature, in reality motherhood *per se* was not the most important part of the matron's life.[50] It is true that cards were sent to announce the birth and again to let it be known that the mother was ready to re-enter Society. But being a mother was certainly not expected to absorb all her time and attention. The physical and emotional care of young children was, in fact, considered to be a distraction from the more important business of wider family and social duties. It is not difficult to read between the lines of such items as this report from a high-class gossip column.

'Lady Beauchamp has a family of young children, whom she adores, and prefers their society and the pleasant surroundings of her gardens at Madresfield and Elmley House to all the amusements of London life. However, this daughter of the Grosvenors does not shirk duty, and had it not been for the sad death of her little nephew, Lord Grosvenor, the series of political entertainments planned for the weeks following the opening of Parliament would have taken place (see section on Mourning). These are, however, only postponed, and will be resumed early in the season.'[51]

Undoubtedly the most demanding stage of motherhood was in the grooming and presenting of her own daughters when they reached their middle and late teens. The relationship of mother and daughter was fraught with difficulties at this stage, partly because the subtle minor rules of the social game changed over the generations. Some women, too, temperamentally disliked these duties and as alternative activities became available this strain was increased.[52] After her daughters were married, or had crossed the rubicon of thirty years and so became confirmed spinsters, the mother could rest on her fixed position as a dowager. Now she had reached the stage where, at least within her own social circle, she could be initiator of contacts with considerable power in her hands.[53] Lord Beaconsfield dubbed people like the Duchess of Sutherland 'social fairies'. They could get ball invitations and other *entrées* for young hopefuls. The formidable mistress of Blickling Hall, 'Queen' of the part of Norfolk surrounding her estate, was nicknamed the 'Double Dow' (Dowager).

Widowhood again changed the woman's status. In fact, the death of any individual changed the status of everyone related to him. In the super-elaborated etiquette of mourning, the Victorians found a superb device in the recognition or non-recognition of kin or friends for placing themselves in the social hierarchy.[54] Mourning for the dead in the form of special carriages, funeral processions with black horses and black feathers had been the custom throughout the eighteenth century. Black clothes had also been worn as a mark of respect. But in the nineteenth century, the etiquette of mourning became much more complicated as it was incorporated into a more formal social code.

The social importance of the deceased was indicated by the degree of mourning: the length of time mourning was worn (and thus restricted social intercourse), the kind of clothing and accessories and the numbers and station of members of the household who went into mourning. As might be expected, widows put on the deepest mourning and wore it for longest. 'First mourning' was worn for a year and a day. This meant black clothes covered with crêpe, no ornaments and a widow's cap with veil.[55] Second mourning then lasted for the next twelve months, black with less crêpe, without a cap and jet ornaments only, called 'slighting' the mourning. The third year was half-mourning when grey or mauve could be added for colour. Some widows chose to remain in mourning for the rest of their lives which could give them certain personal and social advantages. For parents (or children) twelve months' mourning was expected, starting with deep mourning and shedding it by degrees. Grandparents, sisters, brothers, aunts, uncles, cousins and in-laws were mourned in descending order with less time and less crêpe for each category. For the death of the master of the house, servants were provided with mourning caps, gloves and even black work dresses. Children were allowed a little leeway in the use of grey and black ribbons or white clothes trimmed with black.

While in deep mourning, people were placed outside the social world. Close relatives were expected to withdraw from Society for a year. For the lesser categories of mourning three months was a minimum. It was considered extremely bad taste to appear at formal gatherings like balls while wearing crêpe. These were the ideals of the etiquette.[56] In real life they could be used or not with considerable discretion. If there was an important social engagement on the horizon, deep mourning for more distant relatives could be conveniently forgotten. Or if the relationship was denied, mourning could ostentatiously be left off. A passage from a letter of 1850 brings out the use of mourning as social recognition as much as private bereavement.

> Mrs. Whitby was my first cousin . . . but she has lived so long out of the world that I never thought of your mourning for her, or doing so myself although I did seal with black to Emmy.[57]

There must, however, have been times when unavoidable mourning could wreck a well-planned social campaign. On the other hand, friends and god-parents could be mourned through 'complimentary' mourning, as marks of respect and intimacy and so demonstrate membership of a particular social network. The very act of producing a correct mourning—in dress and its accessories, in stationery, seals, floral decorations and other insignia indicated not just the material basis to invest in all this equipment but that the woman was sufficiently initiated into the mysteries of proper mourning to carry it off. The height of the cult was reached about 1870 to 1880, a time of excessive concern with propriety and social placing.

In this social ritual, as in so many others, women were expected to be the chief protaganists and the period of mourning was usually longer for women than for men. After emerging from mourning, the individual or family might have the opportunity to re-shuffle their social hand by the skilful play of cards and calls, especially if their position had been enlarged or diminished by a change in financial position.

The correct use of mourning was also considered part of social duty in order to demonstrate 'decent' behaviour to the working class. Mourning for Royalty including foreign royalty was a symbol of the family-based social loyalties of the upper classes and all those below who identified with them. The Court was looked to for official guidance on mourning ritual although in fact the actual decisions were likely to be made by leading ladies of fashion. When Queen Victoria died in January, King Edward did step in and decree that there should be no mourning after April, otherwise the season could not have taken place which would have undermined the whole fabric of the Society network. Mourning for Royalty emphasised national over class loyalties. Many have written what an awesome sight it was to see the whole of London wearing black the day after Victoria's death, a vast ocean of black, broken only by the white faces under the black hats.[58]

A final note must be added about the interlocking of 'Society' and charity. Most charities were run as private committees. Access to these committees or even permission to do volunteer work at a lower level was in the hands of social leaders although family ties might also be used.[59] Conversely charity work could bring opportunity for mixing with higher social strata as many nouveaux riches families realised. Charity Bazaars, Fancy Fairs, private theatricals, charity garden parties (which were also occasions to show off private homes) were used as money-raising functions to support charitable purposes. But for many people they were seen primarily as part of the season's social calendar. There are many satirical references to the unwanted fancy work, 'tobacco pouches, mufetees, ornamental slippers, watch chains, miles of worsted work' produced to sell at these functions. However, there were so few opportunities for many middle-class girls and women to take part in any sort of organised public event that these functions were highly prized despite masculine ridicule. A sketch of a Charity Bazaar in the 1860s gives an idea of such occasions.

> The bazaar is held in a large marquee, which is furnished by stalls gaily decked out with ribbons, wreaths, and flags, and covered with merchandise; and numberless young ladies preside at the stalls, dressed in the height and breadth of the fashion, and never cease to attract public attention to the goods with the most winning, coaxing, insinuating and if one may be allowed the expression, wheedling ways.[60]

Actual charitable work with the poor was often considered too arduous, contaminating and degrading for young girls to undertake. The administrative side was often in the hands of men. Thus women were thrown back on a very private form of individual help and alms giving, reinforcing the limitations of their social experience, and giving credence to the feeling that the social aspect of organised charitable activity was the most useful and important part. Charity work was part of the wider ideal of social Christian duty. But charitable action should not be carried to excess even by clergymen. In practice this meant that charitable activities should not interfere with establishing a home, entertaining and following the social calendar. It was impressed on girls with all the weight of the dowager's authority that it was their *duty* to appear at balls and carry off gracefully their social role. This divided ideal of social duty came into conflict with enthusiastic reformers, whatever their cause, and particularly the idealistic young who could only cut themselves off from the demands of Society by living in settlements like Toynbee Hall, a choice made only by a tiny minority.

Thus quite genuine conflicts of goals might arise forcing a choice between spending money and time on charity or social activity, since both were legitimately part of a wider social duty. Such conflict left many, particularly girls and women, confused and unable to follow a consistent line of action. Another consequence of the mixture of 'Society' rules with charitable action was to obscure the substantial, often crucial, help given by the working class to each other and to the very poor. This kind of mutual aid had no social visibility and so was very often overlooked and discounted.

By mid-century, the rituals of etiquette and the control of personal life by the rules of 'Society' were accepted in a more or less elaborated form according to the means available, by all of the British middle and upper classes. From Dukes to tradesmen, from village to metropolis, from Inverness to Exeter this unifying system was acknowledged as strictly determining social behaviour.

CHAPTER IV

· ❊ ·

Change and Decline

By the 1880s the basis of London Society membership was beginning to widen. In the sixties and seventies the admission of manufacturers and businessmen of the first and even second generation was problematical.[1] The source of the wealth they had acquired and their route of entry were important elements in their success. Of course, there had always been some rich entrepreneurs or talented entertainers who were admitted to Society without owning land or even a country house. Indeed, their inclusion in socially recognised settings often enabled impecunious insiders to recoup by selling, or at least renting, their inherited landed properties.[2] They had been, however, the remarkable and remarked few.

By the third quarter of the century, the economic base of the landed aristocracy itself began to give way under the effects of the agricultural depression. The amount of wealth became as important a criterion of entry to Society as its source. This shift of emphasis was increased by the introduction of foreign-made fortunes. First were South African and European based families, many of them Jewish, the second wave mainly American. There was a certain amount of anti-Semitic and anti-Yankee feeling resulting from this injection of 'new wealth' into the system but it should be kept in perspective. The whole basis of Society was growing wider and these new very wealthy groups only helped to 'raise the ante' for the material base of operations. The final seal of acceptance, elevation to the peerage, shows quite clearly the shift in recognition. (The table below refers to those from industrial and commercial positions given peerages as well as those nobles and gentry who received peerages *in recognition* of their industrial or commercial achievements.)

Pumphrey assumes that the observed phenomenon of a substantial increase in the number of persons with commercial and industrial backgrounds elevated to the peerage in the middle and later 1880s

Industrialists in the British Peerage[3]

Individuals Associated with Commerce and Industry
Receiving Peerage Titles

Period	All New Peers	Origins in the Nobility	Origins in the Gentry	Other		Total	
				Number	% all new peers	Number	% all new peers
1837–1846	45	0	1	1	2	2	4
1846–1855	19	0	2	1	5	3	15
1855–1866	45	1	2	2	4	5	10
1866–1874	60	1	4	2	3	7	12
1874–1885	69	3	4	1	1	8	12
1885–1895	87	1	5	18	21	24	28
1895–1905	70	2	8	11	16	21	30
1905–1911	65	2	5	19	29	26	40
1837–1911	460	10	31	55	12	96	21

was a lagging secondary reflection of a primary change that had occurred at least a political generation earlier.

At last the ladder of political and social promotion could reach the ultimate goal. In the terminology of the 1860s a 'snob' was a business-man trying to become a gentleman. Those who tried hardest were called 'vulgar' and the ultimate in vulgarity was a 'cad'. Within two generations the meaning of 'snob' was completely inverted. A 'snob' was now any social superior who on a 'false' basis of wealth *or* breed-ing rather than achievement or inherent human qualities, held him-self to be better than those socially below him.[4]

Now the aristocracy and gentry were educating their younger sons for a variety of new occupations. Their family alliances gave these occupations a seal of respectability.[5] Stockbroking, engineering, architecture, certain branches of medicine and new scientific fields were pursued, and in a more expert way, by members of the aristo-cracy giving the lead to talented and ambitious others.[6] Such a process was gradual and not always obvious to the people taking part. Varia-tions in place and personality meant that in some circles, rigid exclusion was still practised often just because a much enlarged and diluted Society presented new problems of definition to both members and would-be members.

Lack of contacts through relatives or a public school background could still be a handicap. Lord and Lady Cowdray, second generation from Yorkshire metal manufacture and immensely rich as well as socially ambitious had a very difficult time in being completely accepted despite their town house in Carlton Terrace and spacious Sussex country home.[7] In the 1890s Elinor Glynn, freshly married into the aristocracy, was coached by Lady Warwick during her first country house hostess season in the Essex countryside:

> Army or naval officers, diplomats or clergyman might be invited to lunch or dinner. The vicar might be invited regularly to Sunday lunch or supper if he was a gentleman. Doctors and solicitors might be invited to garden parties, though never, of course, to lunch or dinner. Anyone engaged in the arts, the stage, trade or commerce, no matter how well connected could not be asked to the house at all.[8]

A writer describing Liverpool at this time says, 'it was a Society wholly independent of London, both more exclusive and more formal, where powdered footmen and knee breeches were still employed for grand occasions in the wealthiest mansions.'[9]

With growing numbers there was also a certain commercialisation and publicity given to social life, changes which were deplored by many.

> Since Society was based on a principle of cohesion which is neither more nor less than a certain *de facto* community of life— that its members have directly or indirectly some social acquaintance with one another and are in the habit of meeting in the same houses or the same resorts, the 30,000 families listed in the Court Guide couldn't possibly take part in Society.[10]

It was estimated that by the end of the nineteenth century there must have been about 4,000 families actively involved, which is probably about the numerical limit for this kind of face to face community held together by gossip and information exchange.[11]

The community feeling, the semi-familial relationships were being undermined. Many contemporaries accused Society of becoming artificial.

> But Society, as it was in this relatively recent past, did not differ from that of today merely in the fact of having been absolutely less numerous and of less multifarious origin. It differed in the effects which a mere restriction of numbers, coupled with inherited wealth and a general similarity of antecedents, has on

the quality of social intercourse itself. In societies which are small, and yet at the same time wealthy enough to secure for their members as a whole a monopoly of varied experience, and invest them with a corporate power which cannot be similarly concentrated in any other cohesive class, these members are provided, like the believers is some esoteric religion, with subtle similarities of tastes, behaviour and judgement, together with daily opportunities of observing how far, and in what particulars, individuals belonging to their class conform or do not conform to them. These are constant provocations of refinements of mutual criticism which give life and conversation a zest not attainable otherwise. Finally a society which is small enough to possess such common standards, and whose position is so well established as to pervade it with a sense that no standards are superior to its own, tends to make manners perfectly simple and natural which could otherwise be approached only by conscious effort or affectation.[12]

In discussing changes which led to greater visibility of upper-class life styles, the importance of photography is worth remarking. In the 1860s and 1870s the process was still being developed; it was an expensive business depending much on the patronage of wealthy enthusiasts. The practice of having Society events photographed caught on quickly and professional photographers followed the country house season as semi-upper servants, keeping records of influential gatherings complementary to the keeping of visitors' books. Later in the century, when photography was cheaper and quicker, the exploitation of 'professional' beauties and personalities in society by photographers accelerated the change to publicity.

Yet another index of growth and complexity was the difficulty in exchanging information by word of mouth only. Printed sources now had to be used. For example the influential magazine, *The Queen*, ran a regular column called 'The Upper 10,000 At Home and Abroad' which listed Society events and their personnel. *The Times* became the local paper for the national elite listing births, deaths, events at Court and so on. By 1910, the semi-annual publication, *Boyle's Court Guide*, announced that 'the dates after certain names (in the alphabetical list) signify the days of "At Homes" ' so that anyone might attend who wished to do so.

There was also an increased commercial exploitation of aristocratic connections. Fashionable gown, hat, lingerie and needlework shops or florists were financed or even run by ladies with aristocratic names to advertise themselves. The owners and managers also used networks of upper-class friends and relatives to patronise them.[13] Another aspect of this process is shown in the magazine article commenting adversely on the following advertisement in a weekly paper:

> A lady in the smartest society in London wishes to chaperone a young lady. Terms £1,000 for one year. Highest references given and required.[14]

Thus guidance in the intricacies of high social life could be bought by the nouveau riche, especially the American variety. It was alleged that some impecunious insiders were even introducing nouveaux riches in return for gifts of carriages, horses or gifts to charity in their name.[15]

The enlargement of numbers taking part in the London season meant inevitably that a certain amount of segregation of social circles began to take place. Beatrice Webb describing London Society as seen by herself as a young girl in the 1880s wrote:

> From my particular point of observation London society appeared as a shifting mass of miscellaneous and uncertain membership, it was essentially a body that could be defined, not by its circumference, which could not be traced, but by its centre or centres; centres of social circles representing or epitomising certain dominant forces within the British governing class. There was the Court, representing national tradition and customs; there was the Cabinet and ex-Cabinet, representing political power; there was a mysterious group of millionaire financiers representing money; there was the racing set . . . All persons who habitually entertained and who were entertained by the members of any one of these key groups could claim to belong to London Society. These four inner circles crossed and recrossed each other owing to an element of common membership.[16]

In this process, much of the political activity of the great houses was lost to the social world. It is true that political parties, particularly the Conservative Party, tended to use the mixture of private friendship, kinship and social activity as a party device for a good deal longer, but slowly Government functions, particularly in the civil service but also in Parliament, became detached from Society. The separation of

Society functions from political office also occurred on the local level. T. H. Escott commented on some of the social effects of the change to elective district councils in 1894:

> Socially, 'the county' continues to exist. The wives or daughters of the country gentlemen who are County J.Ps. set the fashion in their neighbourhood and are still regarded as moulded out of a clay slightly superior to that of which their neighbours consist. But as an object of fetish worship, the County has in most districts disappeared. The tradesmen may be less deferential now that he is a colleague of the squire and magistrate.[17]

J. M. Lee has shown the same process at work at the county level and in the important links of county with national politics in the Cheshire study.[18] Further such studies would show the variation in the way in which the strands of political and social activity were being untwined.

Segregation of social spheres meant it was possible to admit and control certain elements that previously had been defined as unworthy. In addition to new wealth based on trade, the most important of these newcomers were artists and theatrical people. Outstanding and well-patronised artists had always had social access to the great but most often in a patron-client relationship. According to Court etiquette, professional actors and actresses could not be received at Court, nor for that matter could tradespeople. But definitions were elastic and the sponsors or relations of these people might be important enough to smooth over an early career which was not quite acceptable. Once again this demonstrates the flexibility of Society rules, at least in individual cases. But by the end of the century, theatrical people began to be included in the enlarged Society in their own right and on a large scale:

> Sir Coutts and Lady Lindsay's Sunday afternoon parties at the Grosvenor gallery, by personal invitation only, were some of the high points of the season in the 1880s. They took a certain pride in being the first members of Society to bring the people of their own set into friendly contact with the distinguished folk of art and literature.[19]

At a somewhat higher level the Duchess of Sutherland began to hold Friday night salons at Stafford House where 'one saw her entertain a strange and interesting crowd who certainly in early Victorian days would not have been admitted by the grand monde, yet whom

15. Henley Regatta, 1873.

16. Royal Ascot, 1895. The solid iron railings make an intimidating social barrier.

17. (*above*) The Guards Club at Ascot, 1926. The spectators crane for a glimpse of their superiors.

18. (*left*) Inside the paddock, Derby Day 1909. One of Horace Nicholls' excellent pictures of the Society family.

19. (*top right*) Luncheon at Ascot, 1872.

20. (*bottom right*) Luncheon at Ascot fifty years on.

21. (*top left*) Black Ascot, 1910. Lady Knaresborough and her party in heavy mourning for Edward VII.

22. (*left*) Cowes week, 1910. Sir Maurice and Lady Fitzgerald on the landing stage.

23. (*above*) Lady Waldegrave's ball at Strawberry Hill, 1871.

24. (*right*) 'Going down to supper at my first ball', 1890.

25. (*above*) A ball at the Naval College, Portsmouth, 1865.

26. (*left*) The next morning. The lady's maid reads an account of last night's ball to her mistress.

27. (*top right*) The exhausted hostess.

28. (*right*) Going in to dinner.

29. (*above*) 'A dinner party during my first season'.

30. (*top right*) Humility and splendour, 1880. One of George du Maurier's cartoons of the Season.

31. (*right*) The merry-go-round.

34. The quiet family dinner.

32. (*top left*) 'At home'. Note the two young men in the background 'sowing seeds'.

33. A soldier is 'dressed for war' by his adoring women folk.

35. (*right*) A family entertainment. Note the stereoscope the girl is holding in the foreground.

36. (*top left*) A musical evening in the 1850s.

37. (*left*) Below stairs—an imitation of the lady of the house.

38. (*above*) Tea on the lawn. Madame Pavlova's garden party at Hampstead, 1912.

(*left*) Croquet, a very popular game for
~~~ies in the 1850s and '60s.

(*bottom left*) The Archery Club at
~~~nsington, 1906.

(*right*) Golf on the Heath. Advertisers
~~~ quick to seize on respectable ladies'
~~~nes to promote their products.

(*below*) The huntswoman, 1914. This
~~~s originally used as an advertisement for
~~~iman's embrocation.

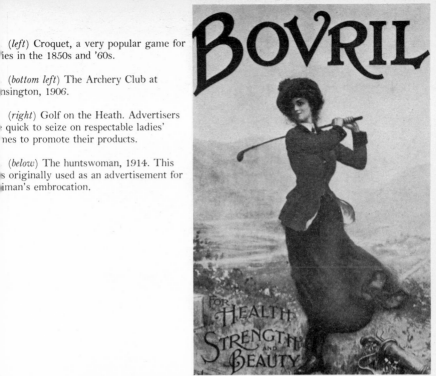

43. A polo match at Hurlingham, 1877, between the Horseguards and the Monmouthshire team.

now the grand monde eagerly flock to meet. Here came beauties, dancers in the Russian ballet, writers, musicians . . . '[20] It should be remembered, however, that although they were now allowed admission it did not follow that all wished to join (see Chapter V).

As political life was segregated from social activity, 'Society' functions came to be regarded simply as a way of life, pleasure as an end in itself with a secondary re-emphasis on the marriage market. It is at this period that Society activities take on more of the 'theatrical' aspect ranging from truly theatrical albeit private productions to pageants through the streets of provincial towns. The following extract gives an idea of the variety and number of occasions the London season could offer. Provincial society tried to follow suit in a more limited form.

To the average man the Season comprises courts, levees, state dinners and balls, Royal garden parties, and a few other events of the hardy annual class, but in reality these are merely the cream of the Season's features. The balls, for example, include private and semi-private dances and the balls for countless charities. The list of dinners, again, comprises innumerable regimental banquets, Empire Day banquets, political dinners, Derby Day dinners, such as that at which the Duchess of Devonshire entertained Her Majesty and thirty other guests in 1907 and afterwards received a thousand favoured friends, county dinners, dinners in aid of charities, and private dinners without number. The receptions, again, are divided up into almost as many classes as the dinners, while the raisons d'être of the numerous conversaziones are almost bewildering in the range of subjects which should, but rarely do, monopolize the conversation. The opera, the theatres, and concerts, sales of work, musical receptions at Mansion House and elsewhere, picture shows, meetings in aids of charities, Congresses, lectures, May Meetings and Primrose League fixtures, exhibitions, the Horse Show, Military Tournament, cricket, croquet, lawn tennis, and other sporting events, bring together great crowds of people interested in these diverse items. The Henley Regatta, the Bisley meeting, Ascot, the Fourth of June at Eton, Speech Day at Harrow, ballooning at Hurlingham and Ranlegh, and countless garden parties, are also important items of the Season that assist to fully occupy the time of those who pursue the giddy round of pleasure.[21]

The pursuit of please for its own sake inevitably meant more emphasis on the young and their flirtations.[22] The emergence of a 'smart set' and such phrases as 'Le Monde ou l'on s'amuse' or 'The Yoke of the Butterflies' date from this time. An Edwardian deb admits that, although occasionally questioning the system which made pleasure a business in a continual round of balls, jaunts, hunting and country house visits, she, being eighteen, took it for granted. 'By just dancing myself dizzy, looking as nice as I could or exploring myself anew through some fresh pair of eyes, I felt I was furthering some momentous, indeed some almost devout purpose.'[23] This was an honest statement of what most middle- and upper-class girls felt, although their society would probably not be on such a grand scale. Another Edwardian deb admits resenting being invited to those parties with a 'heavy political atmosphere'; they were definitely a 'squash'.[24]

The rigid demarcations that had created the Bohemian 'out'-group (see Chapter V) were beginning to be blurred. The Chelsea Arts Ball or Covent Garden Fancy-dress Balls were events that young men from good society might slip off to 'as a joke'. But especially during and after the First World War, dressing up, the tendency to introduce outré clothing and colouring, for example a Russian vogue following the visit of the Russian ballet, began to be used as an excuse for letting even manners, much less morals, relax a little. 'Chelsea revelled in any excuse to dress up and "Society" surreptitiously invaded Chelsea.'[25] But these developments only took place within certain groups. Enlargement and segregation of various 'sets' within Society allowed a certain relaxation in the rigid codes of behaviour that had been demanded at mid-century. One consequence was more toleration of sexual licence within a still very formal social pattern. The phrase 'You can do anything that you please as long as you don't do it in the streets and frighten the horses', was widely circulated.

In contrast, the full force of social propriety fell on the middle classes living in smaller towns or in the suburbs, almost as if they represented a moral backlash to the laxness at the national level.[26] An expected reaction, too, came from some sections of provincial society, aristocratic as well as middle-class. The *Lady* in its Leader for February 1893 pleaded that:

It is a good thing for everyone that there are rules by which Society, now that it has become so vast and complicated a machine, is held together and enabled to work smoothly and

easily . . . it changes very fast and you must keep up with it or
you will stand out and no gentlewoman wants to attract observation or comment or she is not a gentlewoman.

With the dilution and segregation of London Society went a return
to large semi-public functions which were easier for the newly
wealthy to manage, and where more of the plant could be hired for the
occasion.[27] The Prince of Wales reintroduced the masked ball which
indicated that the preoccupation with social identity was no longer so
acute. In the 1890s garden parties became popular functions where
different categories of guest could be included without the implication
that full social acceptance would follow. The ambiguous doctor and
other neighbours could be allowed the semi-privacy of lawns and
tennis court while still being denied the inner sanctum of the drawing-
room. (A social device that has also proved useful to the Royal
Family.)

In all of social life, in fact, there was beginning to be provision for
respectable women to meet in public places outside their own homes.
Cafés, the growth of tea rooms, the use of buses, even the provision of
public lavatories for women, were as important in freeing middle-
class women from strict social ritual as the slow erosion of chaperonage. Contact by telephone and the later mobility that came with cars
began to undermine the most formal parts of etiquette. The telephone
giving direct and immediate access to people in their homes helped to
break down the protection that had been given by cards, calls and
personal servants. Very gradually the game of bridge for older
women and dancing, particularly the tango, for younger ones, re-
placed formal calls and At Homes as major social activities. These
were pursuits that anyone could follow for they depended on skill and
enthusiasm, not social background. In the later nineties and Edwardian period there was a real 'epidemic' of bridge-playing which
swept through the upper middle class with West End clubs catering
for women to play throughout the night.

These social changes were as important in undermining the ideal of
social duty and the domination of the home as the growing claims of
the Suffrage movement. The conflicts inherent in the concept of social
duty were made somewhat more explicit as various forms of social
work became more professional. This was a factor in shaking upper-
and middle-class confidence in face to face dealings with working class
people (see Chapter VI).

World War I almost destroyed the system entirely. Within three years new values for personal life became overwhelmingly important.[28] Prices soared, food and servants were scarce. Charity and war work became substitute places of social interaction for middle- and upper-class women. Even more threatening was the escape of girls from the constraints of the Society path to marriage.[29] By the time peace was declared the new fortunes and new peerages created during the war had diluted the upper class almost beyond recognition. The idea of a 'new rich' and an 'old poor' quickly became social currency, with some truth as the importance of land-owning was finally broken. In 1920, *Ladies Field* desperately extolled the usefulness of *Who's Who* and *Debrett* to keep up with acquaintances, 'especially this year of all years when so many changes in title and position affecting so many people have been made'.

There was a hectic attempt to reintroduce many of the pre-war features of the Season, defending them as a way of presenting a civilised example to other classes and other nations. A simplistic pre-Keynsian economic reasoning was invoked to try to bolster the ideal of social duty.

> The Season as part of our national fabric was refurnished and reborn . . . the English set out to stabilise their national currency, which consists not only of gilt-edged securities but the social system which radiates from their monarchy . . . So when Parliament is sitting, the opera in full swing, *the world entertaining the great world*, the season is of importance not only as the axis of our social stability but as the basis of trade prosperity. London spends and this spending reacts into every industry . . . People who spend benefit every trade. The season is the property of the nation and for that reason, because it is the barometer of prosperity—more than from any social distinction in confers—the world holds on gallantly though purses are slender, taxes high, and estates a burden. The people must live, the shops must sell, the shops must buy, produce and manufacture, and unemployment must be narrowed down.[30]

Court 'Drawing-rooms' became once again splendid affairs, but now the emphasis was very much on the coming out of the young débutantes. Even so, many girls assumed that they would spend only one season as a deb and then take a job, perhaps as a model or in a smart clothes shop. The accent was on entertainment and spectacle,

i.e. the flapper and her attendants. Extensive publicity was given to
Society affairs and their personnel who had started to merge with the
great 'show-biz' community. Cocktail parties and large public balls
given by the new rich were not the places to control entry to this new
breed of elite. For example, in 1928 the 'Great Mayfair War' was
blazoned in the press when Lady Ellesmere of Bridgewater House had
given such a ball. About three hundred guests whom she did not
recognise were present and as an example she had four of them
thrown out. In the following debate, the public was sympathetic to
the gate crashers.[31]

In smaller towns and in the suburbs, the greatest problem in maintaining etiquette was the lack of domestic servants. The women in
these groups, to whom the maintenance of social rules had mostly
been relegated, were very reluctant to give up the attempt even
though they were frustrated at every turn, for no new pattern of
behaviour or social goals had emerged to guide their lives.

Finally there was the problem of the social absorption of the new
groups coming into political power. At the end of the nineteenth
century it had been relatively easy to integrate the small number of
trade unionists and labour leaders via the mechanisms of formal
Society.[32] It was obvious to the newcomers that there were political
gains to be had through social contacts while the more perceptive
social leaders realised that here were important new elements in the
nation's life which ought to be absorbed. For example, the Countess of
Airlie made a special effort to befriend James Brown, an Ayrshire
miner when he was appointed High Commissioner to the Church of
Scotland. She particularly welcomed his wife and helped her with
problems of dress and etiquette encountered in her new position.[33]

But after the war, when there were so many more working-class
representatives and when, above all, their attachment to working class
culture formed their primary tie with their constituents, many refused the blandishments of upper- and middle-class social life. Those
who did not, like Ramsay MacDonald, paid heavily for their
'treachery' in political terms and gained little in return. The bitter
struggles over clothes, for example to possess a dress suit or to wear
a flat cap at all times, symbolised the fact that a group approaching a
powerful political position rejected social integration into the elite,
integration which had always been the strength of English political
continuity.[34] The problems for the wives of the Labour representatives were even more acute. Beatrice Webb, realising this fact,

'probably with recollections of the part played in her earlier days by Mrs Asquith and other brilliant political hostesses' created the Half-Circle Club in London where these women could meet. Although many found these meetings personally enjoyable they never succeeded in making such women socially acceptable, much less a force in politics.[35]

CHAPTER V

·❈·

Variations: Extra-'Society' and Anti-'Society'

The system described thus far might be better understood by looking in detail at groups and individuals who were outside London-based Society. Some were indifferent to national Society having organised their lives around other principles. Others had been denied admittance as undesirable elements, still others were deliberately hostile to Society goals and rituals. Whatever their stance vis-à-vis the system, no individual or group could ignore it completely. All, with the possible exception of the 'demi-monde', had links via family connections with the mainstream of Society at the level appropriate to their economic position, and probably at higher and lower levels as well. For example, most of the Rendel family may have preferred intellectual and welfare pursuits on a Cambridge-Oxford-London axis, despising the worldly Great Uncle whose 'hospitality was invariably directed to the upper strata of politics and Society',[1] but from the Great Uncle's point of view that patticular branch of the family may have been an unworldly embarrassing nuisance.

PROVINCIAL AND SMALL TOWN SOCIETY

Small town Society depended very much on the relation of the local middle class to county groups. Where there was no dominating aristocratic or gentry family or where, as was increasingly the case, the London Season and other attractions of national Society drained away aristocratic attendance and interest, then professional and business people and prosperous farmers took over leadership positions. Those cities with a sizeable wealthy commercial or manufacturing elite differed yet again. Towns like Winchester and Exeter, dominated by a Cathedral, Oxford and Cambridge by their Universities, or

Portsmouth by the Navy had their local Season attached to these
institutions.

In early Victorian times, although all of the middle- and upper-class
groups followed the rituals of etiquette, these circles did not necessarily coincide:

> Lady Catherine had come to Woodeaton as a young bride (in
> the 1840s) looking forward with pleasurable anticipation to the
> intellectual society of Oxford which was only six miles distant.
> But she found to her disappointment that it was not then con-
> sidered etiquette for the County to mix with the University (or
> the City), so she spent a lifetime on the borders of the Promised
> Land only entering it on the rarest occasions.[2]

Later on, these localised societies were swept into the national system. Those that remained provincial tended to be turned over almost
entirely to women. In this way they foreshadowed suburban social life.[3]

Mrs Oliphant, a Scottish emigré transcribing English life with a
somewhat mordant pen, gives a superb portrait of social life in a small
mid-century town.[4] In *Miss Marjoribanks*, one of the Chronicles of
Carlingford, which first appeared as a serial in *Blackwoods* in 1862,
her heroine Lucilla tells everyone that she has come home from school
solely to be 'a comfort to dear Papa'. Papa is a doctor leading a con-
tented life as a widower, who has enjoyed giving his bachelor dinners
for a few cronies for years past. Lucilla turns the house upside down
and puts all her efforts into becoming the acknowledged and absolute
leader of Carlingford. Her Thursday evenings are soon overwhelmingly successful. After ten years of being the 'Queen of Grange Lane'
and yet not having any firm offers of marriage, she realises that her
power has little or no purpose:

> To have control of society in her hands was a great thing; but
> still the mere means, without any end, was not worth Lucilla's
> while—and her Thursdays were almost a bore to her in her pre-
> sent stage of development. They occurred every week to be sure
> as usual; but the machinery was all perfect and went on by itself.
> . . . It was this that made Mr Ashburton's (her candidate) elec-
> tion a matter into which she entered so warmly for she had come
> to an age at which she might have gone into Parliament herself
> had there been no disqualification of sex, and when it was almost
> necessary for her to make some use of her social influence.

Lucilla got her man elected, but in the end she married her cousin Tom who had inherited a small country seat and here, it is implied, she entered her *real* sphere as chatelaine to the estate and political hostess to further her husband's parliamentary career.

Between the extremes of small town or village and the metropolis there grew up the 'burgher' society of the enlarged cities. In some places the local elite seem to have been content with their own Society; small family-based but prosperous businesses were the economic basis for these were self-contained social structures. Is it possible that relative satisfaction with a locally based social life played a part in restricting business expansion, in blunting the desire of the business elite to seek a wider arena? A study of the connection between the local social structure and business enterprise might reveal that what happened in provincial dining-rooms and drawing-rooms was related to decisions taken in provincial offices and board rooms.[5]

When leading families lived in or very near the central city their control over local politics meant that social life was intimately tied to the governing of the city. As families moved out to properous suburbs, local social life centred more on charity, the arts and the marriage market. As Duguid Milne observed (based on his native Aberdeen) as early as 1850[6] it was in the business and professional classes that the separation of the sexes reached a virtual segregation of interests. The centre of the women's existence was not just the home but the home as a basis for social life. And always in the background there hovered the tantalising possibility of merging with county Society, even managing a country house. The close relationship between national Society as experienced in the capital and local variants was not without tensions. In the 1890s a prosperous and socially very successful Hampstead doctor sold up his practice and moved to a small county town. He did this deliberately to cut back expenses incurred by moving in a social set which made it imperative to keep at least four servants and give several dinner parties a week. What he and his wife had not counted on was the exclusion of doctors and other professionals (at least if they were without kinship ties to aristocratic circles) still practised in the smaller more tightly controlled Society of towns such as Hertford. Members of the local elite made full use of his services as a medical man but crossed the street rather than socially acknowledge his wife.[7]

SUBURBAN SOCIETY

The growth of middle-class suburbs created large areas of socially homogeneous populations.[8] This was, indeed, one of their primary appeals. Socially, neighbours and the immediate circle were as important or more important than kin. Socially mobile families, and there must have been many of these, rented suburban houses where it was relatively easy to leave behind undesirable relatives. Conversely, those who had not succeeded wanted also only to mix with their 'own kind'. Control of the social, and thus also, spatial landscape was the very essence of suburban design.[9] The front and back entrance to the house denoted the difference between formal calling and visiting,[10] as well as the watchful control of tradesmen and servants. Hedges and fences as well as nursemaids made certain that suburban children mixed with socially approved others.[11]

The rules of etiquette were strictly observed in controlling contacts and making acquaintances in the anonymous atmosphere of new 'estate' building. A wife from the smaller houses in the area might be invited to the larger house:

> But she would not be honoured by an invitation to the *At Home Day* which might be the Tuesday, first Wednesday, or third Thursday of the month. Not that invitations were issued for such functions. Friends knew that was the day on which the lady of the house was officially at home and it was therefore good form to call. She would inform new acquaintances whom she considered worthy, what her 'Day' was. It was also engraved on her visiting cards—and visiting cards were essential then. Knowing the day and being sure you would be welcome or at least expected you called as if duty bound. The residents of the lesser roads knew all about these days, they had their own—but they never called then. They knew they were not of the inner circle. When they called it was on an 'off' day and by appointment. They had tea downstairs from an earthenware teapot, not in the drawing-room from the silver teapot.[12]

Very often a tennis or other club would be used as the social centre where a mini-season of activities including the presentation of local girls took place. Or for those living in the suburbs of London the national Season could be followed by attending some of its more accessible functions like the Opera, Boat Race or Ascot, although only in the public areas not private enclosures. Society activities could also be followed in the press. For example the first issue of the monthly *Home Life—A Publication for the Home Circle* in 1890 said in its opening editorial:

> We propose to provide in crystallised form, news of the doings of ladies in Society and the World whose position, characters and endowments make their lives interesting to their less prominent and their less distinguished sisters.

Even in the very wealthy suburbs, public activities seem to have centred on charity and cultural affairs rather than political concern with city government.[13] And here too social life was almost entirely in the hands of women. (See Appendix for similarities to the American pattern.)

ALTERNATIVELY BASED SOCIETY: RELIGIOUS MINORITIES

At the beginning of the period, Nonconformists as a whole, but particularly the stricter sects like Quakers, tended to mix socially only within their own ranks. This was partly because they had, for the most part, urban or commercial origins and Liberal political affiliations at a time when these were still barriers to full social acceptance. But it was also because many sects had their own equivalent of the 'Season'; for instance the Quakers had their yearly *Meeting* in London where family and social ties were renewed and new alliances made through marriage.[14] Later on, when national Society had become more centralised and dominant, many individuals or even whole families quietly crossed into the established Church, some for admittedly social reasons.

Catholics, after the Act of 1827 allowed them seats in Parliament, found no legal barrier to full participation although many chose to confine themselves to Catholic churches and local county affairs.[15] This served to maintain the hegemony of Catholic families, one factor reinforcing the other. 'At any entertainment given at a Catholic house, the bulk of the guests—perhaps three-fourths of them—would be Catholics. These would be people so closely connected with one another by blood or lifelong acquaintance as to constitute one large family.'[16]

Jews found more official bars to full membership. But even they, by the end of the century, could enter Society by accumulating great

wealth and adhering to the rules of etiquette and gentlemanly behaviour.[17] In fact England, compared to other European countries, for
example, Germany, was remarkably open to all these minorities.[18]
The existence of a formal sifting institution like Society *encouraged*
such openness. As with the other minorities, it was as much cohesion
within their own group as exclusion by the wider society which kept
Jews from being completely absorbed in the social mainstream.[19] The
consequences for English political life of such an open system can be
calculated by comparing the position of Jews on the Continent.
Michels, in discussing the formation of the Socialist leadership in
Germany and Eastern Europe, says:

> Even when they are rich the Jews constitute a category of
> persons who are excluded from the social advantages which the
> prevailing political, economic and intellectual systems ensures
> for the corresponding portion of the Gentile population. Society,
> in the narrower sense of the term [Society] is distrustful of
> them . . .

He then goes on to argue that such barriers to full acceptance
made it easier for bourgeois Jews to abandon their class of origin and
identify with the socialist movement.[20]

ALTERNATIVELY BASED SOCIETY: THE 'INTELLECTUALS'

Some families whose values were expressed in activities where
political power was not important played down participation in the
rituals of Society. The most interesting example yet examined in
detail is Noel Annan's 'intellectual aristocracy'.[21] Their spiritual forebears can be seen in the Clapham Sect, whose incomes were securely
bulwarked on small capital investments. In their pursuit of scholarly,
scientific and literary aims they could afford to belittle the worldliness of Society.[22] Within their own ranks such groups could provide
the intellectual and social background for success in their chosen
sphere. As Annan shows, they could so afford to make their *cause
célèbre* open competitive examinations for the Civil Service and
University positions. They used the competitive system to gain
visible rewards for *achievement* in membership of the newly created
learned and professional bodies.[23]

In one sense, access to their ranks was more difficult than the more
formal Society. It was harder to gain the ease of manner, culture and

bearing which alone gave admittance to membership of these circles than it was to go through the formal ritual of Society. On the other hand while to maintain a position in Society it was necessary to keep up a front, among this group, once a member was adopted, either by establishing a distant cousinhood or by marriage, he would be supported and helped even in adversity. The awkward duller schoolboy would be given a temporary post as private secretary to some outstanding personality in order to develop his confidence and bring him forward. A nascent, and possibly mediocre, talent in the arts would be cultivated to its full in constant contact with the most distinguished practitioners. A niche could usually be found for everyone.[24] A good example of such a family can be found in Baroness Stock's autobiography. Her mother was one of eight brothers and sisters, all of whom lived in or near Bedford Square and Gordon Square. They had 'At Homes' on alternate days so that they met as a family virtually every day. The grandparents' country house in Surrey was used as a headquarters and holiday home for numerous family members. They were quite proud of their ignorance of much of the ritual of Society and etiquette. Another well-known description of such a 'connection' or cousinhood in action is the portrait of the Darwins in Cambridge by Gwen Raverat.[25]

With cousinhood support, with a better education than most of their contemporaries and freed from the demands of formal Society it is not surprising that so many politically and economically pioneering women came from this group.

ALTERNATIVELY BASED SOCIETY: CLERGY AND 'BOHEMIANS'

There were certain occupations whose system of values might conflict with the demands of Society. The clergy, especially after the reforms of the 1820s and 1830s, who took their Christian duties seriously were often in a dilemma.[26] In order to be effective in ministering to their poorer parishioners it was imperative to use social contacts with middle- and upper-class patrons. But this was extremely time- and energy-consuming and laid them open to the charge of worldliness. The conflict between these values fell especially hard on the female relatives of the clergy. Of course there were many, like some of the more renowned 'squarsons', whose lives were completely absorbed in the social and sporting round. Fortunately for them the social week, no matter how worldly, always ended with church on Sunday. Even avowed agnostics usually admitted the social duty of church attendance.

Creative artists were in a rather different position. Many remained through the nineteenth century in more of a client relationship to their wealthy patrons than free social agents. Some followed conventional customs and, on becoming very successful, had considerable contact with upper-class individuals who found sorties to St. John's Wood an enjoyable change from the usual social activity. The official ideology might maintain that all artists and actors were suspected of undermining respectability; in fact, success and wealth could bring compensations.[27] On the other hand, some artists used their calling to turn their backs on formal society and mix only with their own kindred spirits as, for example, the Pre-Raphaelites, part of whose charm was in the deliberate rejection of Victorian social conventions.

The concept of Bohemianism reflects this definition of writers and artists as those who were seen, and saw themselves as outsiders, foreign to normal society. Thackeray uses the word 'Bohemian' in 1848 to refer to a wild roving girl whose parents where actually gypsies. Later the word 'Bohemian' came to mean, as one Victorian accurately though awkwardly said: 'That section of Society which lives out of Society.' By mid-century 'the world', having been defined, or rather self-defined, as those who lived within the rules of etiquette, all others must live outside that world.

> Curious that there should be men [*not women*, author], who never enter a drawing-room, or leave a card or make a formal call, or go to Church, or subscribe to anything or attend funerals, or give anybody in marriage, or are godfather to anybody's child, or are executors and trustees to anybody, or are consulted about anybody's education, or take the chair at public meetings or are generally respected in any 'neighbourhood known as the grave and busy and polite world at large'. It is to their complete alienation from all this that such men owe the appellation which assimilates their class to that of the gypsies. He is not among us, he is a gipsy *ipso facto*.[28]

UTOPIANS AND REBELS

Other groups inspired by religious or political ideals also rejected the conventions of Society and etiquette. Their goals included the meeting of individuals as equals, direct contact without the interminable intermediary of ritual. But this rejection tended to cut off their financial as well as social lifeline to the wider society and was one of the reasons for their usual failure to survive as a viable group.[29]

On an individual level, some rebelled by becoming explorers of other ways of life either at home or abroad. Edward Carpenter passionately loathed the proprieties and rules of his middle-class home in mid-century Brighton.[30] He, and later others like Stephen Reynolds, escaped these constraints by living with working-class families or individuals. Mavericks like Richard Burton, the explorer, anthropologist and linguist, turned to other cultures abroad.

Individual wriers often found difficulty in placing themselves in relation to Society. Trollope's case is well known through his autobiography. John Galsworthy, too, was a writer who could recoil at the excesses of the system but who was also fascinated by it. His novel, *The Island Pharisees*, published in 1908, chronicles the journal of a middle-class young man who was an outsider to Society. The chapter titles: Society, Marriage, Settlement, The Club, The Dinner, The Wedding, Rotten Row, At Home; indicate his progress. Further study of outsiders and deviant cases would highlight what was expected of the conforming majority.

Among even this majority, there was also a sub-stratum of individual behaviour which can be seen as a reaction to the rigid control of everyday conduct necessitated by the rules of Society. Violent, even macabre, practical joking and house party 'romps' including kissing games while couples hid in wardrobes hardly fit the stereotype of Victorian behaviour but they are frequently mentioned in memoirs. Some of this behaviour can be regarded as sheer high spirits breaking through what had become intolerable restraint. But some of the inconsistency in applying sanctions to the breaking of conventional rules might be better understood if it is remembered that the rules were being used to protect the social fabric; personal morality was secondary.

It should also be kept in mind that this kind of rule can be invoked as part of a power struggle within a small group like the family or household. For example a girl may have been told by her parents that a suitor was unsuitable on social grounds when in fact their real reason for rejecting him was their unwillingness to release the girl from their own control.[31] But in any case it is obvious in this context that rebellion was more difficult for women than for men. The characteristic way of punishing transgressions against the code was to cut the parties involved (whether or not they were 'guilty'). Since women had no alternative institutions or groups with which to identify they could only react to ostracism by personal eccentricity or even physical collapse. Invalidism was a way out of social as well as family obligations. There is a Victorian horror story about a jealous newly married husband who destroys his wife's identity by hiding all cards and invitations that come to the house. Driven almost insane by this mysterious rejection, when she discovers what he has done, she actually poisons him in revenge.

As far as daily life for the majority, however, it took only a very little breach of etiquette to feel thrillingly wicked.

> There were so many of these little rules to remember, but we were drilled (by Nanny) so that it was no effort to remember them and, indeed, a breakage of any one of them meant conscious and premeditated rebellion.[32]

THE 'DEMI-MONDE'

The system that has been described was intensely formalised and hierarchical. And yet it was used to promote a great measure of social fluidity. The individuals taking part in such a system inevitably are concerned with problems of closure especially at the lowest levels where the lower middle class merges with the working class. It was among these groups that gentility was most nearly equated with the idea of respectability, and for women, respectability was nominally equated with sexual respectability.[33]

Sexual respectability could only be maintained by being identified with a home, a family status. The fear of women being enticed into uncontrolled social as well as sexual relationships literally cut them off from any existence outside their homes or homes of relatives and friends. Etiquette books and manuals reflect this identification of social acceptability with physical place.[34] In his chapter on 'The Etiquette of Places', the anonymous writer of the 1840s says:

> Nowhere has a man or woman occasion more frequently to exercise the virtue of courtesy than on the street; and in no place is the distinction between the polite and the vulgar more marked . . .[35]

It has been argued in Chapter III that marriage meant the establishment of a home and a social status as much as a sexual union. It may even be that the reaching for unrealistically high standards of sexual 'purity' was a reaction to the potential of social mixing. No women who appeared in 'public' could be really respectable no matter what her actual sexual behaviour. This attitude may help to explain some of the ambiguity felt towards actresses.

In this context, it is instructive to look at the career of 'Lily' Langtry. She started life unexceptionally respectable as the daughter of the Dean of Jersey, Rev. William Corbett La Breton. After an early marriage to an unknown member of the Irish gentry the couple came to London and were introduced into 'Society' through a tenuous connection with a member of the aristocracy. Charm, beauty and personality made her quickly accepted and she entered fully into a round of fashionable pursuits including private theatricals. She was persuaded to act in semi-public for a deserving London charity and 'the performance was witnessed by the elite of the fashionable world and a very considerable sum of money was raised for the charitable undertaking'. But the next step, to becoming a *professional* actress, would never have been taken by Mrs Langtry except for sudden bankruptcy and desperate need for money.[36] Members of the upper and middle class found her fascinating simply because she had crossed this social rubicon.

Another consequence of this doctrine was that working-class girls who had no recognised family to protect them, in other words no social place, could be, and often were, open to labelling as prostitutes or at least 'fallen' women, no matter what their behaviour had been. For example, an abandoned twelve-year-old girl who had been wandering the countryside with an itinerant musician was automatically assumed to be a young prostitute and sent to a Penitential Home. Thus marked, she found it very difficult to make her living in domestic service.[37] The obsession with defining women solely by their status within the family may help to explain the antipathy of the middle and upper class to girl and women factory workers; the resentment and outrage at their 'independence'. The factory was seen as, above all, an uncontrolled public place. Therefore it was an unnatural setting for women and would inevitably lead to sexual immorality. The fact that working-class men and women did not, indeed could not, have these same attitudes was incomprehensible to middle-class moralists, and this incomprehension extended to other aspects of

6

working-class personal morality as well as attitudes towards women's work.[38]

The very nomenclature of Victorian respectability reflects an obsession with order in social relation to which untamed sexual attachments were so threatening. A woman who was accused of transgressing the code of respectability was 'fallen' i.e., dropped out of recognised social life. The institution of the 'demi-monde' implied a twilight social world that existed without the controls of etiquette.[39] The female inhabitants of this world are often described as 'shades', 'ghosts' or 'shadows' in both fiction and journalism. The discussion of reclamation work among fallen women is full of allusions to 'lifting', 'bringing back', 'helping up' from an anonymous outer Hades into the recognised social world.[40]

In actual fact, thousands of girls and women went through phases of prostitution and returned to respectable life when they married or they could find other work.[41] Such facts were, however, not only unacceptable but unimaginable to most Victorian observers. It took a Herculean leap in imagination to see that it was domestic servants, considered the most protected of working-class girls living as they did in private homes, who were in fact the most vulnerable recruits to prostitution.

Although there was so much casual prostitution, it is true that the threat of permanently losing one's place in respectable society was a very real one. Once labelled as a fallen woman, it followed that the chances for tolerable service in the case of working-class girls or marriage in the case of middle-class girls were much reduced. Only those few professional prostitutes who had reached a fairly high social and financial level could ignore Society definitions of 'in' or 'out'.[42] For there was a hierarchy even within this twilight world. Victorian writers are vague about the level at which courtesans ended and prostitutes began. They were all 'fallen' of course, but some were more fallen than others. For instance, Gladstone, in his reforming zeal, seemed to prefer 'going for "those at the top of the tree" '.[43] Indeed at that level a mild flouting of 'Society' rules had its attractions. Towards the end of the century, the minor novelist, G. J. Whyte-Melville, who had a very sharp eye for the social scene, described a young widow who ran her home as a comfortable gathering place for sophisticated Londoners.

Now Mrs Montpellier was one of these ladies on whom their

own sex choose to look somewhat askance without any defined cause. There were certain houses to which she was asked, certain people with whom she interchanged the card-leaving and other dreary courtesies of society; but those who repudiated her averred that the houses were what they called 'Ominum Gatherers' and the people 'second rate'. 'Who is she?' demanded Lady Visigoth—who are her antecedents? There are stories about her.' Mrs Montpellier, twice widowed, came back from India and made her house the pleasantest lounge in London. She saw a great deal of very agreeable society. If you were dying to meet "somebody" and dined with Mrs Montpellier you were sure to go down to dinner with that "somebody" and no other on your arm.'[44]

SOCIETY ABROAD

Whyte-Melville makes this socially ambiguous woman appear on the scene 'recently returned' from India, and this device was used often by novelists with good reason. An elaborate structure like London Society, whose personnel was increasingly interchangeable with country house Society, needed places and times where individuals and families could get away, to recoup themselves, or if they wished, drop out of the system all together. Psychologically and physically the easiest way to do this was to leave the country.[45]

There were three categories of 'abroad' in English life at this time. There was colonial Society where the occupants of Government House were automatically defined as the leaders. The permanent official hierarchies of Colonial Office and the Army, combined with the presence of vast subject populations completely cut off from social contact, made Colonial Society an even more rigid inflexible system than the one at home. The greatly imbalanced sex ratio in the colonies also meant that while men could choose to live outside it, 'going native', the women became its fanatical protectors.[46]

In contrast to this situation there were the dominions, particularly Australia, where all the Government House protocol could not really combat the equalitarian ideals, sparse population, rugged conditions and lack of servants which emphasised informality and an easy-going social atmosphere. In much of the literature about Australia and Canada coming from middle-class women's emigration societies, emphasis is placed on the benefits of being able to give up dressing and acting like ladies when one hadn't the means to do so.[47]

The third area abroad was continental Europe. There was an official Society to be found in all the European capitals connected with European Courts. Indeed, one of the attractions of being presented at the Court of St James was the automatic entrée it gave to foreign Courts. But there were also English communities in almost all European towns of any size. Here social life was much more easy-going. Without formal appearance to maintain, real financial re-trenchment could be effected.[48] A mid-Victorian who had married into a Swiss patrician family and gone to live in Zurich told her niece that she was 'shocked to find that nobody dressed for dinner except on special occasions'.[49]

By living abroad social faux-pas could be smoothed over and even illegitimate babies could be born and left behind. For example, when a country rector had a clandestine affair with a middle-class girl living in the vicinity, 'the girl went ostensibly for a trip to India, which was another name for a maternity home'.[50] And when Henry Thornton outraged Society by marrying his dead wife's sister, he and his new wife fled abroad. He conducted his parliamentary campaign to chal-lenge the illegality of this type of marriage from the safety of the Continent. The couple returned in the summer following their marriage on what they called an 'experimental trip' in order to see how many people would call on them.[51]

CHAPTER VI

Women and Work

The consequences of such a rigid code of behaviour imposed on a large and influential sector of the population were, of course, manifold both at an individual and group level. Undoubtedly, the firm belief in this code very much coloured the attitude of the upper and middle classes to the personal behaviour of working-class individuals, an area of contact between classes which needs more much study.[1] In this discussion it is only possible to refer very briefly to four areas of social life most affected by the paramount ideals of social duty manifest through Society and the Season: housing, domestic service, household management and the behaviour of middle- and upper-class women.[2]

HOUSING, SERVANTS AND HOUSEHOLD MANAGEMENT

The emphasis on the home, not just as a symbol of the family's social standing but as a complicated basis of operations for the business of Society, had several important effects on middle- and upper-class housing throughout the period. Until World War I, all but the small group who inherited or bought country seats and a few of the very wealthiest families who owned their town houses, *rented* their homes.[3] The complicated tradition of leasing (unfurnished tenancies of three, five or seven years) which is part of the British land tenure pattern meant that superficial renovation and decoration were left to the tenant, but the landlord had little incentive to make structural renovations or to rationalise services. This may have been a major factor in the reluctance to install better plumbing, heating and lighting systems. Houses continued to be rented because a good deal of social mobility was literally mobility from area to area. If retrenchment or advancement in the scale of social life was wanted, the family moved. If desperate they could take lodgings, i.e., part of someone else's house.

Secondly the migration during the Season meant a heavy demand for town houses during three to five months and very little demand during the rest of the year. Those who lived in London all year round, however, were affected by the same market factors and landlords who could make a great deal of money during the Season by redecorating the main reception rooms were little inclined to improve kitchens. In the year of Queen Victoria's marriage, 1842, when demand for town houses in London was even higher than usual, a lady from the north trying to bring out her daughter during the Season wrote: 'Finally we discovered a very small house in Chesterfield Street to be still unlet, probably because it was so ridiculously expensive at thirty-two guineas a week.'[4]

These seasonal fluctuations in the market also affected provincial centres like Edinburgh, Dublin, York, Exeter and Norwich as well as seaside or spa towns like Bath, Brighton, and Harrogate. Provincial cities as well as London were affected by the overwhelming importance given to a proper address from which to launch Society functions, and thus also professional and business connections. In London the domination of Mayfair and Belgravia as a desirable location was only broken because the pressure of numbers finally spilled over into Kensington and then Bayswater although for a long time they were not considered quite as correct.[5] Further down the scale the same considerations had much the same impact on housing stock. Mrs Panton, a well-known late Victorian writer on household management complained about the inconvenience of houses but she admits that 'neighbourhoods alter so rapidly in character and in *personelle* likewise, that I cannot blame young folk for refusing more than a three years agreement, or at the most a seven year's lease'. She advises against the longer lease for then the landlord can insist on redecoration and all sorts of 'absurd renovations'.[6] Conventional expectations hampered those who were looking for a simplified style of life. For example a family in straitened circumstances after prolonged illness and death of the father could only visualise the mother and three grown-up daughters living together in a full establishment of a 'house in the country' with stables, gardens, etc., that they couldn't really afford.[7]

The internal arrangements of the house were even more affected by the type of living dominated by Society considerations. The same passion for control through categorisation and segregation of populations and functions as that found in Victorian public institutions

coloured the ideal of the gentleman's house.[8] The servants' department, the children's segregated quarters of night and day nursery
kept non-participants out of sight and hearing.[9] The transition to
adulthood for girls was thus partially an actual physical move from
nursery to schoolroom, punctuated by a complete change of times
and settings for meals. The ladies' boudoir, the smoking-room (and
in larger houses, the billiards and gun-room), the guest suites with
separate staircases for bachelors and unmarried women ensured that
even full participants interacted only in set places at set times.

The physical setting for the rituals of calls, At Homes, teas,
dinners and balls was extremely important.[10] On the largest scale, this
included an entrance dominated by a lodge, gates and a drive.[11] At a
less elaborate level, the front steps and front door furniture displayed
the rank of the householder and required much attention from
domestic servants, for example, the specially hired 'step girls' employed in middle-class suburbs. All business and trade inquiries went
to the back door. The front door was opened by a servant correctly
mannered and dressed to suit the status of the family. The hall, and in
larger establishments, special ante-rooms, were used to 'hold' the
caller in limbo while the servant went to find the required member
of the family in the private regions of the house. In larger houses, the
Servants Hall was sometimes used to hold special categories who were
halfway between back and front door status, e.g., the doctor, schoolmaster, important tradesmen or unimportant kin. These neutral areas
were organised and controlled by upper servants (or possibly semi-
familial dependants like a poor relation-cum-housekeeper) *not* family
members who were protected by space and time-lapse from initial
contacts with outsiders.[12]

Within the body of the house, pride of place was given to the drawing-room, dining-room and hall through which the dinner procession
passed. The subdivided offices and attics for supporting or non-
functionary groups: servants quarters, nursery and schoolroom for
older children, formed a myriad of small dark rooms opening from
extra staircases and corridors. The primacy of social goals produced
houses which, as Mark Girouard has said, are less congenial and less
useful to us than the open, airy houses of the eighteenth century.

As housing was arranged to present the family socially to the greatest advantage, so were the servants, both in numbers and quality. For
example a Victoria was well known to be a carriage used by the not
quite so well off because it could be driven without a footman. A lady

creating a new social set on arriving in London declared that she would not call on any household who 'only had a parlour maid' in place of men servants.[13] Even in single-servant, middle-class homes, social presentation was considered vitally important. In women's magazines, for example, there is constant reference to the fact that the first appearance of the footman or parlourmaid at the door reflected the family's rank and quality. 'A Lady in Society' approvingly quotes Ruskin as saying[14] 'The black battle stain on a soldier's face is not vulgar but the dirty face of a housemaid is.' When out calling, the footman carried the lady's cards to the receiving servant at the door who then announced whether or not the family member was At Home. The discretion of a good servant was important in this subtle fiction in the game of social barriers. Such 'front-stage' servants were deliberately chosen for height, good looks and clear speaking voice, qualities which effectively barred the promotion of girls from poor backgrounds especially workhouse girls.

Because these servants were seen as an extension of the household 'aura', they were deliberately depersonalised, hidden under standardised liveries and and often called standardised names, e.g., Thomas and Susan, whatever their real names might be. Well-trained upper servants could be hired by the nouveaux riches to teach them the subtleties of upper-class life. In this way, a newly enriched family could hire a whole establishment of house, gardens, stables, groundsmen and servants which served as a stage set for their performance in Society. The analogy between a theatrical performance and Society functions is very strong. Upper servants were aware of this. They knew, too, their power in the production of these performances and could use this power to balance a relationship which usually had the dice loaded heavily on the employer's side. 'So much depends on the constant cooperation of well-trained servants. Without it, the best bred of hostesses is placed at a disadvantage.'[15]

Lower servants cleaned and maintained the elaborate physical plant which was the setting of Society events. The chef or cook on the kitchen side, the housekeeper, butler or head housemaid on the house side directed and organised all these diverse activities which were aimed at producing not only smoothly running family life but the more frequently dominant goal of a successful social life.

Servants had to accept their duties no matter how irrational they might seem. They often did not understand or accept the goals of middle- and upper-class social life and saw through attempts at presenting a front to Society with too scanty resources. A woman who was in service about 1908, in a hardworked, two-servant place, recalls that she had to be in afternoon uniform on duty on the day of the regular At Home. She was expected to answer the door as well as make the tea refreshments which included 'thin rolls of bread and butter'. She resented the expectation that she could be in two places at once. She says:

> 'and the funny thing was they used to leave their cards on a tray on the hall table, I think it was—I don't know why, but one of her own cards and two of her husband's—visiting cards—so that each lady would leave three. Goodness knows why.'
> 'What happened to the cards?'
> 'Oh they were collected, I suppose. Anything very important they used to leave there so that people could see it I think . . . there'd be sometimes seven or eight ladies. Hers (At Home) was the first Tuesday of the month. *It was all so shabby.*'[16]

After World War I some of the bitterness in the employer/servant relationship was due to the increased questioning of formal social life, entailing as it did sacrifices of servants' individuality and comfort. Inevitably higher costs and less materials meant heavier work loads. But many employers still tried to carry on the system as before.[17]

In most families, both men and women gave top priority to the production of social performances at whatever level they could manage.[18] In the highest spheres this could mean a very elaborate set constructed at great cost.

> I realised that the pursuit of pleasure was not only an undertaking but also an elaborate . . . undertaking, which entailed extensive plant, a large number of employees and innumerable decisions of insignificant matters. There was the London house to be selected and occupied; there was the stable of horses and carriages to be transported; there was the elaborate stock of prescribed garments to be bought; there was all the comissariate and paraphernalia for dinners, dances, picnics and weekend parties to be provided. Among the wealthier of one's relatives and acquaintances there were the deer forests and the shooting-boxes, all entailing more machinery, the organisation of which frequently devolved on the women of the household.[19]

Such priorities often ran counter to the wish for privacy, purely family life and/or literary or scientific avocations and public or charitable works. Throughout the period there were debates about these conflicts of interest[20] but in practice social goals usually took precedence. Then too, the overlapping of kinship and social networks helped to blur the boundaries between familial and social duties.

The general acceptance of these priorities meant that household management was, in a technical sense, 'irrational' if the physical servicing of the residential family with food, clothing, warmth and hygienic facilities had been given first place. 'Comfort' in British homes meant an abundance of space in order to segregate categories of people and an abundance of personal attendance rather than 'creature comforts' produced by the least wasteful use of materials and division of labour, as transatlantic visitors were often quick to point out. For example, it took the typhoid epidemic of the 1870s drama-tised by the near death of the Prince of Wales to force even wealthy householders to face the problems of indoor sanitation.[21] Servant power was squandered on hours of polishing silver, or brass door handles and stair rods and producing a surface polish rather than real cleanliness.[22] A household where there was a lady's maid to pack, do the hair of the mistress and grown-up daughters and wait on them, a butler to open the door and pour the wine, could still be actually dirty. In such a house the children scampering up and down staircases and passages used to discover what they gleefully termed 'filth packets' behind furniture, in drawers and cupboards and various odd corners.[23]

House design included yards and yards of extra corridor and stair-case which ensured ceremonial segregation but also doubled work loads. Even without the extra catering for guests there were basically three sets of meals served four times a day in the most ordinary households: servants, nursery and adult family. This could be elaborated to separate meals for kitchen, servants' hall and house-keeper's room, nursery and schoolroom, late breakfasts merging into special luncheons, drawing-room teas and late dinners, until the staf-fing and organisation required could have easily run a medium-sized hotel. The display of china, pictures, furniture, hangings, knick-knacks and cushions hampered even the most enthusiastic housewives. The resistance to using more efficient hot water and heating systems surely had more to do with this preoccupation with the ceremonial side of family life than with some mystical facet of British national character (as changes in the last few years have shown).

The constant shifting from place to place demanded by the Season's activities meant a great deal of time and manpower was spent on packing and unpacking great trunks of clothing, baskets of plate, cutlery, crockery, nursery equipment (down to the portable tin bath), the pets, the sketching material, the sporting gear. Very often upper servants were sent ahead to smooth the journey or would accompany family members to wait on them in transit. When many such moves were made each year, a high proportion of servant time could be absorbed in the mechanics of moving. Then there was the constant but irregular influx of house guests and guests for meals so that the household plant had to have a much larger capacity than for ordinary family use. Much of this plant was often idle but still needed basic cleaning and servicing throughout the year. Rigid standards and inflexibility connected with vague notions of duty, added to these irrationalities of scale as many a kitchenmaid or housemaid could have testified when, for example, they were forced to do such extra jobs as washing a 100-piece best dinner service every week although it might have been in use only once every six months.

About 1900 a few brave souls started to question these priorities. There was some attempt made to simplify social and family life. But even the 1918 War, followed by a severe housing and servant shortage, as well as very steep inflation, did not completely do away with the struggle to keep up late dinners and ceremonial calling.[24] Recalling this period Enid Starkie says of her mother's attitude to economy:

> She genuinely believed that our high standard of living—of the gestures of living rather than its enjoyment—was absolutely necessary, that it was part of the self respect arising from our social position, part of the necessary fulfilment of our duty to society, a duty which we could not avoid . . . The main consideration in my mother's mind was that others should not realise what had happened, should not guess our difficulties, that there should be no suspicion of a smaller and a meaner life.[25]

Her mother was convinced that if this became known it would jeopardise her husband's career, but also that she herself would not be able to maintain her sphere of action in Society. She genuinely believed that the new dresses, the cut flowers, the parties were expenditures for her family and her class rather than herself.

Given this attitude it is not surprising that a rational attitude to household arrangements was difficult if not impossible. Although lip service was paid to the importance of a knowledge of housekeeping for upper- and middle-class women, the concept of social duty reflected in elaborate entertainment was still in direct competition with the demands of housework and child-rearing.

In 1846 the American ambassador's wife wrote home that

> The subjects of conversation among women are more general than with us, and they are much more cultivated than our women as a body . . . they never sew, or attend as we do, to domestic affairs and so live for social life and understand it better.[26]

In 1870, M. Taylor, a writer on women's affairs, endorsed this view:

> As her means increase every wife transfers every household duty involving labour to other hands. As soon as she is able to afford it she hires a washer-woman occasionally, then a charwoman, then a cook and housemaid, a nurse or two, a governess, a lady's maid, a housekeeper—and no blame attaches to any step of her progress, unless the payment is beyond her means.[27]

Indeed, it was her duty to free herself for a higher sphere.

This attitude remained substantially unchanged until the Second World War. It has had overwhelming consequences for the teaching of domestic skills, the technology of housekeeping and house design which, in turn, have directly affected working-class family life.[28]

WOMEN

The exhortations to women to act as guardians of the domestic hearth, so typical of early and mid-Victorian writing, refer to an entity wider than the immediate or even extended family. It has been argued that the physical and social location of Society activities had to be the private home, no matter how small the scale might be. Men, especially middle-class men, had to leave the home for the struggles of the market place, or to take their part in the armed services, the Church and politics. So the custodianship of the *turnstile* (Lady Jeune) that was Society fell to the women. Just at the time when men were learning to perform new, more professional tasks either in completely new businesses and professions or within older but transformed institutions such as the armed services and government, women were forced back into operating in a more narrowly personal and private sphere. The consequent differences in attitudes which I have indicated in Chapter III began to be formed in childhood. Not only was most of the content of a girl's education aimed at accomplishments (foreign languages, dancing, music and drawing) useful only to the Society sphere, but the setting—the private governess teaching only the girls of a single household—helped to mould attitudes and behaviour patterns suitable to the girl's future role.

An educational sociologist has argued that the classroom situation creates certain 'psychological capacities' that give children 'the abilities to engage in non-familial types of authority relationships and to govern one's conduct by the norm of universalism'.[29] Leaving home and embarking on graded tasks in the company of thirty or more peers of equal status and equal responsibility 'provides the first prolonged experience of impersonality', teaching children how to deal with segmented attention, how to sever relationships without feeling personally bereft. In multi-servant households, with the attendance of Nanny, nursery maid, governess, ladies' maid, footman and butler, as well as parents, grandparents, aunts, uncles and family friends there simply did not exist any setting where Victorian upper- and middle-class girls could measure themselves against this kind of experience; the typical small private boarding and finishing schools were hardly substitutes.

Instead their 'career' line depended on using every personal attraction they could to reinforce what status they inherited through their family in order to manœuvre a marriage and thus gain the first rung on the ladder of Society. The strict demarcation by age as well as status of women and girls in the nineteenth century is indicated by the variety and complexity of their clothes as opposed to the almost uniform dark 'workman-like or business-like' look of men's clothing after the 1840s. Every cap, bow, streamer, ruffle, fringe, bustle, glove and other elaboration symbolised some status category for the female wearer; mourning dress being the quintescence of this demarcation. A footman, with long experience in upper-class households, said 'jewellery was a badge that women wore like a sergeant major's stripes or field-marshal's baton, it showed achievement, rank, position'.[30] It is not surprising, then, that girls and women of all classes were preoccupied with dress.

As I have shown, public attention in Society went to the married women and any real power to influence the social circle came rather late in the woman's life. The supreme authority of the dowagers, who set many of Society's rules, made it an extreme trial for a girl to attempt an alternative path. One woman recalls her reactions to these formidable social leaders at a ball in her youth.

> I often felt worthless and out of place and any charm or useful-
> ness I had in daily life, was vanishing like a wraith of mist in a
> chill wind . . . the serried ranks of dowagers sitting bolt upright
> on gilded chairs or sofas round the room underneath glittering
> chandeliers intimidated much bolder spirits than mine.[31]

Thus there was a general but personalised surveillance of every step she took. The fact that social pressure was often brought to bear on her mother and other relatives as much as on herself made the psychological burden even greater.

Because their economic position as well as social status was completely dependent on home affiliations, girls and women were particularly vulnerable to sudden financial shifts due to changes within the family. These might include not only the well-known sudden penury through the death or failure of the male breadwinner but also sudden elevation such as the necessity of becoming an official hostess in a large organisation; for example, if her husband became a local dignitary, a church official, an administrator in some far-flung post of Empire or inherited a country estate. Reference has also been made to the breaks in a social career made by suddenly enforced mourning.

And of course, if the woman or girl were suddenly faced with loss of income there were, in effect, no viable economic alternatives. The conditions of chronic underemployment and exploitation among governesses and lady companions were recognised even among Victorians. The whole question of paid work for middle-class women in the nineteenth century is more understandable once the primacy of social goals is admitted.[32] The occupations which were suggested as suitable for gentlewomen were often only makeshifts for ways in which a lady might add to a small income. They tended to be in the personal service area, depending heavily on the use of friends as clients or customers. Hand books and magazines list such occupations as cleaning jewellery, dusting rare china and furniture, walking, clipping and washing dogs in the client's own home; possibly being a peripatetic lady cook. An article advises letting one's own town house during the Season and taking a country house with garden near a railroad station. Then the lady might raise flowers and fruit, bring them up to town and do some table decoration for friends.[33] No men-tion is made to financial support for the rest of the year, or the intense competition which such endeavours would meet from trained gardeners and upper servants. The hopelessly trivial, marginal and unremunerative nature of such work is evident but as long as social demands required women to remain in a private setting and out of the labour market there were no real alternatives. The complete failure of the attempt to use 'lady helps' as upper servants hinges on this fact. The underlying attitude is made explicit in a letter to the *Englishwoman's Journal* of 1866:

> My opinion is that if a woman is obliged to work, at once (although she may be Christian and well bred) she loses that peculiar position which the word *lady* conventionally designates.[34]

Married women, too, had no legal right to what income of their own they might possess and even after the passing of the Married Women's Property Acts, little customary right. All these factors taken together weave a pattern which offered very limited scope for control over their own life chances despite, in some cases, considerable material wealth.

These 'psychological capacities', early experiences, and career expectations for girls and women remained essentially unchanged over the period under discussion, but the sphere of activity in Society did not. Early in the century, when the small Society of the day was intimately linked to political functions, great power as well as pleasure could be derived from the system. The zest and enjoyment of such a life can be sensed from the memoirs of the Countess of Brownlow who was first her father's and then her husband's hostess, moving in the highest political and social circles.[35] Or again in mid-century Anglo-Indian Society Mrs Richard Strachey was happiest while her husband was on active duty in India.

> Her chief passion in life was public affairs. Allied by birth and marriage to the aristocracy of Anglo-Indian families, the daughter and wife of great administrators, a profound interest in the craft of statesmanship was inherited in her blood and fostered by all the circumstances of her life.[36]

Her return to English society of the 1880s was a return to a much more circumscribed existence. By that time the potential for power offered by gaining and holding a place in Society was not as great. New opportunities and other spheres of action for women had also tempered the climate of Mid-Victorianism. But it was a slow process.

In the 1840s the force of sanctions brought to bear on girls or women who were really not fitted for or refused to accept the priorities laid down by Society were very severe. These sanctions are illustrated in the well-known case of Florence Nightingale.[37] Her rejection of marriage, it should be noted, was not a rejection of marriage as a sexual relationship or Richard Monckton Miles the man, but was specifically a rejection of continuing the round of social duties. In the 1840s it took the forces of a religious call and near insanity to break from this assignment. Yet several generations later, for many girls, the demands of Society still appeared to be in direct conflict with the nascent women's professions. For example, during the Boer War, untrained women went out to South Africa at their own expense to nurse the wounded and at the same time carry on their social round. The few professional nurses trying to work alongside this kind of amateur found their job made very difficult. In the nineteen hundreds, Eva Hubback was an enthusiastic Fabian and helped in an East End settlement. Yet 'it did not seem to her at all curious to combine her work in Whitechapel with the social round at home. It certainly would not have occurred to her to give up the latter, for she accepted the fact that while she was living in her parents' home she should take her proper place in helping them to entertain and in being entertained herself. She had no idea of treating her work in Whitechapel as a profession.'[38]

Such situations could create genuine conflicts of loyalty. Too often they have been written off as examples of female instability, the fluttering of social butterflies. In fact it might be argued that the very existence of some alternative activities or even occupations made the girl's position more uneasy. Vaguely she might wish to do 'something else', realising that Society activities were less attuned to serious affairs, but the means, the skills needed to make such a change were beyond her reach. The effort needed to rebel against personalised familial authority was too great.

My own double mind was the real trouble during these years. I did not care enough for social life to work at it—to improve my dancing, to listen to boring partners as if they were interesting, to keep my weight down and take trouble to dress well on a moderate allowance. Yet I had not the resolution and steadiness of purpose to find a line of my own and pursue it.[39]

In the 1890s, Mary McCarthy, whose father was headmaster at Eton, trying to find something more satisfying than the social duties she saw her mother perform, announced that she wanted to be a Sanitary Inspector and tried to study for the exams on her own. Her parents gently laughed at her: 'I'm afraid, darling, it is most unlikely that this will come off. You will have to resign yourself always to being an English lady, doing one thing at one time and another thing at another.'[40] She failed the examination.

The Suffrage Movement gave some women experience of public organisation. More, however, tried themselves in the still semi-familial organisations attached to the Church which had widened its activities to include lay workers by the end of the century. Even this limited introduction to public organisations was a trial to many.

> In 1915, Lady Addington recalled how difficult the early Girls' Friendly Society associate (upper-class women) found questions of procedure and management. 'It *was* a great and somewhat mysterious attraction in the seventies, and I well remember how interesting it was to go to one's father for instruction in the intricacies of "taking" a meeting.'[41]

But until and even after the First World War the opportunities for organised *impersonal* action were few and candidates for office often unsure of themselves and their goals. For, in the last analysis, the skills required for middle- and upper-class life-style rest on the ability to manipulate face-to-face relationships rather than achievement in any 'universalistic' sphere. Skill in organising the household, or the money to pay for someone else to do it, were necessary as a base for performance but far more important were charm and awareness of other people.

Emily Eden in her novel *The Semi-Attached Couple*, written about the 1830s, describes the problems of the mistress of a country house who had the servants, family and guests under her 'sovereignty'.

> She . . . had heard the history of the contretemps of the morning and was prepared to pacify, and explain, and smooth, and conciliate till all should be peace again. Such is the daily toil of the mistress of a large country house. No laundress, ironing away at an obstinate row of plaits; no carpenter planing the roughest plank of wood; no gardener taking the stoniest soil, has half the trouble she has, to maintain a smooth surface in the

7

aspect of her mixed society. Nothing more is asked. They may all hate, all envy, all rival each other; they may say everything that is ill-natured, and do everything that is mischievous but the 'general effect' must be harmony; and this must be maintained by the tact of the hostess.[42]

One hundred years later, Virginia Woolf describes, more subjectively, essentially the same situation in a scene round the dinner table. Mrs Ramsey, the hostess, tired after a day spent 'ironing out' difficulties among her family and guests, looks round the room as the meal starts:

> Nothing seemed to have merged. They all sat separate. And the whole effort of merging and flowering and creating rested on her. Again she felt, as a fact without hostility, the sterility of men, for if she did not do it nobody would do it, and so, giving herself the little shake that one gives a watch that has stopped, the old familiar pulse began beating, as the watch begins ticking —one, two, three, one, two, three . . .[43]

Most men could choose whether or not to enter Society. In any case, those who had other occupations to perform could use their wives (or sisters, daughters) to represent them. The great majority of women had no choice. The results were, as expected, a 'failure of nerve' on the part of most women even when given the opportunity for achievement.

Under similar conditions, such expectations imposed on even a most privileged status group, *male* aristocrats, could produce a similar reaction. Chester Kirby asks, 'Why Dukes and other ranks of the British Aristocracy have not produced "greatness"?' He answers himself:

> On the whole it seems to be essentially true that to be born heir to a dukedom is a bad way to begin life if one wishes to climb to the pinnacles of lasting fame. He dominates what he surveys, loaded with titles, demanded as chairman and subscriber for every occasion and every charity. He has to give his attention to a million affairs of business . . . In short he must be everywhere, slight nobody, encourage everybody, which is to say he must scatter his efforts and live the life of a Jack-of-all-trades.[44]

If this was true for dukes and lords, how much more so for upper- and middle-class women who had to cope with the added burden of repeated childbearing?

The insistence on women remaining private, or at least amateur figures, explains some of the contradictions in the nineteenth-century record. In fact, girls and women were attending lectures and classes at Oxford in the 1870s.[45] They were even casting votes in local elections. But they were doing all these things in a *private* capacity. Those whose private resources were great, for example, someone like the Duchess of Sutherland, were able to operate in a wider sphere, automatically assuming leadership positions in voluntary bodies such as the Red Cross. It was middle-class women without resources and barred from public positions who were at the greatest disadvantage.

By the inter-war period, the reduced scale of living for most of the middle class, the decline of chaperonage and new freedom for girls, meant that even the 'career' sequence of schoolgirl, deb (or provincial variant), daughter-at-home, matron and dowager wielding power in the social/political world, had ceased to have much cogency. In June 1920, a rather plaintive article in *The Lady* says:

> It appears that paying and receiving calls was a consolation to the middle-aged woman. The young are taken care of under the new happy-go-lucky system. They have relieved their parents of any responsibility for finding them amusement and making friends for them. The parents being left without these duties find themselves at a loose end. Is there, after all something to be said for reviving an institution to which Red Cross and other war activities dealt a death blow? Or would it not be better for the lonely middle aged to think out some other scheme for social amenities? An afternoon call is rather a frigid business.

It is possible that the turning inwards to motherhood and domesticity in the 1930s was partly caused by a decline in Society functions. It is interesting that the magazine *Good Housekeeping*, introduced from the United States in 1922, gave most emphasis to technical household skills and mothercraft. The woman is now seen as guardian of her family's health and happiness rather than of its social place.

A lack of confidence in the idea of social duty begins to be apparent about this time. The changes brought about by the war were partly responsible and to these were added the growing depression of industry and trade, unemployment and the challenge of Keynsian economic explanation. The statement of alternatives presented by socialism had penetrated even the most protected and isolated middle-class homes; no matter how violently they were rejected they did pose an alternative idea about the role of upper- and middle-class life styles. This lack of confidence undermined the morale of middle-class women just at the time when housing, material and servant shortages made the struggle to carry through the round of social duties—paying calls, acting as social leaders in community activities and charities, maintaining a formal, ritualised pattern of life—infinitely more difficult. The slightly mocking self-deprecatory tone of E. M. Delafield's *Diary of a Provincial Lady* which first appeared as a very popular series of articles in *Time and Tide* in the late 1920s catches this mood:

> Undoubtedly a certain irony can be found in the fact that I have recently been appointed to the new Guardians Committee, and am expected to visit Workhouse, etc., with particular reference to children's quarters, in order that I may offer valuable suggestions on questions of hygiene and general welfare of inmates. Can only hope that fellow-members of the Committee will never be inspired to submit my own domestic arrangements to similar inspection.[46]

The Second World War effectively broke the hold of Society over individual lives. An official Court Circular of 1958 admits that 'since the last war "Society" in the sense in which it was known even in 1939 has almost died'.[47] Levees for the presentation of men were discontinued and only débutantes could be presented and then in parties, not individually. In 1957 even these presentations quietly ceased. After almost one hundred and fifty years—and five generations later—the remnants of Society, like the trappings surrounding diplomacy and the monarchy, are for the most part theatrical productions.[48] Attempts to resurrect part of the ritual produce only a synthetic imitation.[49] Yet this system, based on a life-style of leisure, sport and the pursuit of elegant social interaction in the past has been the model for all but a minority of the upper- and middle-class as well as having had irresistible fascination for many working-class women.

In the present current climate of uncertainty about the relationship of individuals to larger units of society in general and the family in particular, it is vital to have some understanding of what has gone before.

APPENDIX

·❈·

'Society' in Two Other Cultures

A brief look at the experience of two other countries may be of interest in contrast to nineteenth- and twentieth-century Britain. At the one extreme is a patrimonial society like pre-revolutionary Russia; at the other is the open society of a western American city. How did social relations among elite families function under these circumstances?

The aristocracy in Russia in the 1860s and 1870s was still supremely untouched by industrialisation or the claims of a nascent middle class. All of its assets and its values were connected with land ownership. Within their town and country houses, large numbers of servants, retainers and poor relations slept in halls, antechambers or even behind screens in the huge drawing-rooms. In contrast with the rigid timetabling of social gathering and meals in the British household, the table was always set in readiness for some meal. Furniture tended to be functional rather than for decoration.[1]

Moscow and St Petersburg were still unsophisticated cities with no particular fixed Season of events. Formal invitations were only issued for important dinners or balls. Otherwise the old custom of 'tapers' was used. Those wishing to receive callers would set a candle in the window. Any acquaintance passing by could call and know he would be welcome. If individuals or families felt like visiting they would send a servant out to get a list of 'tapers' and then choose the most congenial neighbour or friend to call on. Such a system could only exist where status was visibly fixed.

In America the older colonial areas had a system of etiquette similar to the mother country. But the lack of an acknowledged aristocracy or national centre such as the Court made their attempts at creating substitutes, e.g., the Boston 'Brahmins' the First Families of Virginia or the Philadelphia 'Main Line' somewhat strident in comparison.[2] It also furthered exclusion on ethnic and religious grounds. Later on when new wealth came very quickly to many unknown families even more artificial attempts were made to create enclosed status groups, the most famous being Mrs Astor's Four Hundred in New York. In a similar vein, many cities tried to introduce Blue Books, i.e., lists of socially acceptable names chosen by committees of social leaders.

Those who felt they were eligible for entry on the basis of wealth and achievement but who were excluded on grounds of religion, ethnic background or race, formed their own Society.

More significantly, American Society did not intermesh with politics as it did in England. As a result it 'was run almost entirely by women, with the same spirit of competition which aggressive males display in business. There were no true salons for the four hundred were not, as in England, a political ruling class, concerned with the obligations as well as the "perquisites" of power.'[3]

The lack of access to real power through Society meant that its reward and entertainment function was stressed. Moving to the more open society of the middle-west this phenomenon can still be seen at work in St Louis, Missouri. Here in the eighteenth century the French settlers formed the original elite. Nineteenth-century German businessmen became the nouveaux riches in the post-Civil War expansion. In an effort to wrest social recognition for their contributions to the city from the French they created the *Veiled Prophet* and his *Retinue* which combined an annual spring *Mardi-gras* procession and festival with a Ball where local débutantes were presented to the Veiled Prophet. To be his maid-of-honour is still the local girl's highest aim. Dinners, dances and all the other paraphernalia of Society centre round this institution.[4]

By contrast the more wealthy and sophisticated Americans of the East Coast and the South in their search for a truly honorific life-style, 'opposed to the claims of sheer property' (Weber) turned nostalgically to Europe and the English peerage in particular. A description of Society in Mobile, Alabama, in the 1850s gives the highest accolade in comparing the local elite (whose wealth was based solely on commercial trade in cotton) with the European aristocracy:

> Many families it is my happiness to know are not surpassed in high breeding and truly elevated character by the best class of English society; and this is saying a great deal; for I look upon the *best* society in England as the best in the world.[5]

From the later part of the nineteenth century through the 1920s this quest for true aristocratic status produced a series of great 'international mergers' through marriage. The introduction of wealthy American women into England at the end of the century was one of the factors making London Society more spectacular but also less rigid and exclusive.[6]

NOTES

---·❁·---

CHAPTER I—INTRODUCTION

All books are published in London unless otherwise stated

1. J. Banks, *Prosperity and Parenthood*, 1954.
2. W. J. Reader, *Professional Men*, 1966.
3. Thorstein Veblen's explanation of conspicuous leisure and conspicuous consumption seems over-simple. In any case he bases it on his American experience. T. Veblen, *The Theory of the Leisure Class*, New York (1899), 1965.
4. Some examples: U. Bloom, *Victorian Vinaigrette*, 1956; R. Harling, *Home: A Victorian Vignette*, 1938; J. Dunbar, *The Early Victorian Woman*, 1953.
5. There is a difficulty in deciding how to designate Society in print to distinguish it from the more general sociological concept of society. In fact, the word was not used in this special sense, i.e. meaning 'the aggregate of leisured, cultured or fashionable persons regarded as forming a distinct class or body' (*O.E.D.*) until the first quarter of the nineteenth century. It first appeared in this sense in Byron's *Don Juan* in 1823 and undoubtedly grew out of the contemporaneous concept of a conservative organic unity in the social body; a concern with maintaining standards and resisting demands for change. The resulting somewhat confusing designations, Society and society are not, therefore, accidental. I have decided to use Society throughout the text to distinguish the one from the other.
6. Gillian Avery, *Nineteenth Century Children: Heroes and Heroines in English Children's Stories, 1780–1900*, 1968.
7. W. L. Guttsman, *The British Political Elite*, 1963.
8. F. M. L. Thompson, *English Landed Society in the Nineteenth Century*, 1963.
9. Partial exceptions are the excellent analysis of a local scene, J. M. Lee, *Social Leaders and Public Persons: A study of County Government in Cheshire since 1880*, 1963, also D. Spring, 'The Role of the Aristocracy in the Late 19th Century', *Victorian Studies*, September 1960.
10. Max Weber, 'Class, Status and Party', in H. Gerth and C. W. Mills (eds.), *From Max Weber: Essays in Sociology*, 1948, p. 192.
11. Charles Kadushin, 'Power, Influence and Social Circles, A New

Methodology for Studying Opinion Makers', *American Sociological Review*, October 1968, p. 169.

12. For some information on the change in women's position see Ivy Pinchbeck, 'Marriage, a Business Partnership in the Eighteenth Century', *Women Workers and the Industrial Revolution*, 1969.

13. T. C. Smout, *A History of the Scottish People*, *1560–1830*, 1969.

14. H. Perkin, *The Origins of Modern English Society*, *1780–1880*, 1969.

15. The effects of these developments on family life in the working class have been studied in M. Anderson, *Family Structure in 19th Century Lancashire*, 1972.

16. The Victorian middle-class home as a bulwark against social chaos has been convincingly portrayed by Barbara Frankel. I am much indebted to her excellent analysis. However, I am arguing here that the home was more than just a centre of defensive family interaction and was part of the wider system of Society. Barbara Frankel, 'The Genteel Family: High Victorian Conceptions of Domesticity and Good Behaviour', unpublished Ph.D. thesis, University of Wisconsin, 1969.

17. I have not attempted to discuss the place of the public schools in the amalgamation of elites and their relation to Society. It has been argued that the public schools were effective in introducing middle-class boys to their aristocratic counterparts as well as giving them a common social background. In this way the schools could have taken over some of the functions performed by Society. R. H. Wilkinson, 'The Gentleman Ideal and the Maintenance of a Political Elite', in P. W. Musgrave, *Sociology*, *History and Education*, 1970.

18. Viscountess Rhondda, 'Leaving School and Coming Out', *That Was My World*, 1933, p. 93.

19. One of the most popular series was published by Warne, written by an anonymous 'Member of the Aristocracy'. They included *Manners and Tone of Good Society* (in its 24th edition in 1911), *The Management of Servants*, *Party Giving on Every Scale*, and *Society Small Talk*, *Or What to Say and When to Say it*.

20. Including interviews from 'Family Life and Work Experience Before 1918', the survey being carried out by Paul and Thea Thompson, University of Essex.

CHAPTER II—SOCIETY AND THE SEASON IN THE NINETEENTH CENTURY

1. G. Mingay, *English Landed Society in the 18th Century*, 1963.

2. An outsider like Disraeli was fascinated by this system as he shows in both *Conningsby* and *Endymion*.

3. Quoted in G. Rudé, *Hanoverian London 1714–1808*, 1971. p.144.

4. The process, still going on in the third quarter of the century, is described

in M. Carberry, *Happy World, The Story of a Victorian Childhood*, 1941. She was the daughter of a younger son. Her father and four friends, all bankers, discovered Coombe Wood in Surrey and all built houses there. When they gained peerages they called it (facetiously) 'coming out noble.'

5. E. Barber, *The Bourgeoisie in 18th Century France*, Princeton, 1955.

6. W. L. Guttsman, 'The Decline of Aristocracy', *The British Political Elite*, 1963.

7. Asa Briggs, *Victorian Cities*, 1963.

8. Ivy Pinchbeck, 'Social Changes in the Farmhouse', *Women Workers in the Industrial Revolution*, 1250–1850, 1969.

9. Mark Girouard, *The Victorian Country House*, Oxford, 1971, p. 4.

10. P. Aries, *Centuries of Childhood, a Social History of Family Life*, New York, 1962.

11. Mary Cholmondeley, *Under One Roof: A Family Record*, 1918, p. 3.

12. M. Girouard, op. cit., 1971.
The dullness this could produce did not go unremarked: Mrs Ward, 'A Country Dinner Party', *Ainsworths Magazine*, Part 14, May 1842.

13. Brian Harrison, *Drink and the Victorians*, 1971, p. 304.

14. John Howard 'The Season', *Belgravia: A London Magazine*, June 1871.

15. J. Ashton, *Social England Under the Regency*, 1899.

16. A. Thirkell, *The Fortunes of Harriette*, 1936.

17. 'Side Scenes of Society', *Punch*, 1843, p. 59.

18. Major A. Griffiths, *Clubs and Clubmen*, 1908.

19. At the club, a good hall porter should know everybody and everything. He played much the same part as the head footman who opens the door at a private house. R. Neville, *London Clubs*, 1911.

20. 'Presentation at Court' (mimeographed circular from the office of the Lord Chamberlain). 'In the Royal Library there is a Wilke drawing depicting an Afternoon Drawing Room at Holyrood House in 1822 with the ladies in feathers and trains and the procedure indistinguishable from that of an Evening court.' (The latter took place as late as the 1920s.)

21. Lord Chamberlain, op. cit.

22. 'Man of the World', *Court Etiquette: A guide to Intercourse with Royal or Titled Persons to Drawing Rooms, Levees, Courts and Audiences and the Usages of Social life, c.* 1850, p. 32.

23. M. Jeune, 'Political Great Ladies', *The Realm*, April 15th, 1895.

24. O. W. Hewitt, *Strawberry Fair: A Biography of Frances Countess of Waldegrave 1821–1879*, 1956. Her own social background should have disqualified her from even entering 'Society' on at least four criteria. Her father was Jewish, he had made his fortune as a concert singer and he had an acknowledged illegitimate son by his mistress before marrying her very middle-class mother from Manchester. The force of her personality and her alliance with the aristocracy through marriage overcame these handicaps.

25. The boom in country house building continued up to the 1880s. M. Girouard, op. cit., pp. 5–6.

26. Lady Tweedsmuir, *The Lilac and the Rose*, 1952.

27. F. M. L. Thompson, op. cit.

28. 'Before a man could become a Justice of the Peace he had to win social acceptance into the ranks of the gentry, which was no easier for him than it was for the shopkeeper's wife to take tea with the doctor's' . . . But if and when, at long last, the gentry did pay calls on the urban squire he 'still had far to go before he could realise this fondest wish.' E. Bovill, *English Country Life 1780–1830*, 1962, p. 75.

29. Chatsworth, the country house of the Duke of Devonshire, had a special theatre gallery with permanent stage and seating. The impact of private theatrical productions on the public theatre is an interesting subject in its own right.

30. Which can be seen as analagous to the process in the working class. M. Anderson, *Family Structure in 19th Century Lancashire*, 1972.

31. E. Bancroft-Davis, *Letters from England 1846–1849*, 1904, p. 114.

32. Isabel, Marchioness of Aberdeen, *The Musings of a Scottish Granny*, 1936, p. 86.

33. Racing at Goodwood started in this way. Lady Muriel Beckworth, *When I Remember*, 1936.

34. Isabel, Marchioness of Aberdeen, op. cit., 1936, p. 60.

35. Whyte-Melville, Surtees and Trollope have provided abundant literary data on the importance of hunting in the social game. Norbert Elias discusses the uniquely English use of sport in elite life-styles in 'The Genesis of Sport as a Sociological Problem' in E. Dunning (ed.), *The Sociology of Sport*, 1970.

36. Some girls and young women hunted and rode with a passion that amounted to mania. As far as I can tell this was not censured or seen as antithetical to the proper performance of social duties.

37. Richard Doyle, *Bird's Eye View of Society*, 1864, p. 13.

38. G. Whyte-Melville, *The Brookes of Bridlemere*, n.d., includes a realistic description of this at the 'Middleworth Ball'.

39. P. Bottome, *Search for a Soul*, 1942.

Throughout the century there were even very eminent men who, despite their close involvement with politics, disliked Society and London life, preferring their estates and families. For the early period see:

     Denis LeMarchant, *Memoir of John Charles, Viscount Althorpe, Third Earl Spencer*, 1876,

     G. M. Trevelyan, *Lord Grey of the Reform Bill*, 1920.

For the later part of the century:

     Lady G. Cecil, *Life of Robert, Marquis of Salisbury*, 1921.

40. John Littlejohn, *Westrigg: The Sociology of a Cheviot Parish*, 1963, pp. 56–57.

41. David Jenkins, *The Agricultural Community in South West Wales*, Cardiff, 1971, p. 35.

42. F. Hodgson-Burnett, *The Making of a Marchioness*, 1901.

43. Michael Young and Peter Wilmott, *Family and Kinship in East London*, Institute of Community Studies, 1957.

44. W. H. Mallock, *Memoirs of Life and Literature*, 1920, p. 70.

45. H. G. Wells, *Tono-Bungay*, 1909, Penguin ed. pp. 80–81. Even acceptable hotels were 'private' and required personal introductions to gain admittance, i.e., Claridges, Browns.

46. Emily Charlotte Langtry, *The Days I Knew*, 1925, p. 108.

47. M. J. Gifford, *Pages from the Diary of an Oxford Lady 1843–1862*, 1932. Lady D. F. Allen, *Sunlight and Shadow* (Rhodes House), 1960. G. Huxley, *Lady Denman, C.B.E., 1884–1954*, 1961. John James, *The Memoirs of a House Steward*, 1949.

48. John Burnett, *The History of the Cost of Living*, 1969.

49. Emile Durkheim, *Suicide: A Study in Sociology*, Free Press, N.Y., 1951, (1897), p. 252.

50. B. Frankle, op. cit., 1969. (These principles as applied in public institutions can be followed in some of the debates on the new Poor Law, 1832.)

51. George Moberly, born 1803, whose father was a merchant engaged in foreign trade, was one of eleven children. Between them they had 93 children and 256 grandchildren. C. A. E. Moberly, *Dolce Domum: George Moberly, His Family and Friends*, 1911.

52. The novels of C. Yonge are revealing on this point. The Yonges were close friends and neighbours of the George Moberlys and their fifteen children.

53. B. Howe, *A Galaxy of Governesses*, 1954. One of the more spectacular results of these reforms in personal behaviour was the decline in drunkenness in all classes. Brian Harrison, *Drink and the Victorians; the Temperance Question in England, 1815–1872*, 1971.

54. It is difficult to date the habit of changing into evening clothes for dinner, but it was certainly a firmly fixed custom by the end of the 1860s.

55. E. P. Thompson has discussed changes in conceptions of time as they affected the working class in 'Time, Work Discipline and Industrial Capitalism', *Past and Present*, no. 38.

56. M. Jaeger, *Before Victoria*, 1946. M. J. Quinlan, *Victorian Prelude: A History of English Manners 1700–1830*, 1941.

57. The absence of sumptuary laws was both symbolic and helpful in this amalgamation.

CHAPTER III—THE ANATOMY OF SOCIETY AND ETIQUETTE

1. Virginia Woolf, *Orlando*, 1928 (1970), p. 176.
2. M. Weber, 'Social Strata and their Status', in *The Theory of Social and Economic Organisation*, 1947 (ed.), T. Parsons.
3. John Russell, Duke of Bedford, *A Silver Plated Spoon*, 1962.
4. Margaret Lane, *The Tales of Beatrix Potter*, 1968.
5. Or at least to husband your resources while waiting for a rise in income, e.g., 'Climbing the Hill: a story for the Household', which appeared as a serial in 1866.
6. L. Potter, *Lancashire Memories*, 1879.
7. A two- or even three-generational process which has similar consequences for family relationships in any newcomer group seeking acceptance in a host society. Oscar Handlin, *The Uprooted*, New York 1951.
8. Discussed in B. Frankle, op. cit. This belief flourished partly because of the visibility of Society spending. It was estimated that by 1900 Ascot cost £175,000 or £2,900 per minute of actual racing.
9. 'Is Society Worse than it was?', *Nineteenth Century*, January, 1903.
10. Mrs Peel, the writer on household management in the late 1880s and 1890s was a very sympathetic and intelligent social observer. She defends the idea of 'social duty' in her autobiography but admits to an uneasiness when faced with its full implications. D. S. Peel, *Life's Enchanted Cup 1872–1933*, 1933.
11. N. C. Geary, *The Law of Marriage and Family Relations—A Manual of Practical Law*, 1892.
12. See the analogy with J. Dollard, *Class and Caste in a Southern Town*. Two recent books fit in with this speculation. D. Hudson, *Munby, Man of Two Worlds: the Life and Diaries of Arthur J. Munby, 1828–1872*, 1972, and E. M. Forster, *Maurice*, 1972.
13. W. Mallock, op. cit., p. 73.
14. J. Wildeblood and P. Brinson, *The Polite World: A Guide to English Manners and Deportment from the 13th Century to the 19th Century*, 1965.
15. Anonymous, *How to Behave—A Pocket Manual of Etiquette*, Glasgow, *c.* 1860.
16. Mrs John Sherwood, *Manners and Social Usages*, New York, 1899.
17. This type of explanation seems to me much more convincing than various invocations of national character usually put forward to explain differences in behaviour at this level.
18. Maude C. Cook, *Manual of Etiquette or Social Forms, Manners and Customs of Correct Society*, 1896.
19. K. Chorley, *Manchester Made Them*, 1950.
20. *The Lady, a Magazine for Gentlewomen*, February 9, 1893.
21. Maisie Ward, *Unfinished Business*, 1964.

22. Lady Colin Campbell, *Etiquette of Good Society*, 1911, p. 63.

23. *The Queen*, October, 1895.

24. 'In County Society' by Au Fait, *The Queen*, September, 1912.

25. In a sense these printed sources helped create the phenomena they were supposedly explaining. This is, of course, quite a common feature of modern societies with mass circulation of newspapers and magazines. See Cynthia White's *Women's Magazines 1693–1968*, 1970. I am indebted to her for the use of some of her original notebooks.

26. Paul and Thea Thompson, op. cit., Interview.

27. G. Stedman Jones, *Outcast London: A Study in the Relationship Between Classes in Victorian Society*, Oxford, 1971, pp. 34–35.

28. How to Behave, op. cit.

29. Attempts to introduce less formal (and less costly) evening social activities were not very successful except among artistic, literary and other 'outsiders'. Lady St. Helier, *Memories of Fifty Years*, 1909.

30. Sir Bernard Burke, *The Book Of Precedence. The Peers, and Knights and the Companions of the Several Orders of Knighthood Placed According to their Relative Rank*, 1881.

31. Gwen Raverat, *Period Piece: A Cambridge Childhood*, 1952, p. 78.

32. J. Ellis, *Thatched with Gold: The Memories of Mabel, Countess of Airlie*, 1962, p. 158.

33. Christopher Isherwood, *Kathleen and Frank*, 1971, p. 111.

34. Prince Pückler-Muskau, *A Tour in England, Ireland and France in the Years 1828–1829*.

35. G. Curtis, *A Chronicle of Small Beer; The Early Victorian Diaries of a Hertford Brewer*, 1970.

36. The Knutsford County Assembly Ball which was the apex of the Cheshire gentry's social calendar, had always been divided on the basis of small house parties. The invitations were sent to the head of the household who then chose his own group of guests. J. M. Lee, *Social Leaders and Public Persons*, 1963.

37. W. Besant, *Fifty Years Ago*, 1888.

38. *Work and Leisure*, 1882. The implication that marriage was used as a social status as much as a sexual union is reinforced by the use of the courtesy title 'Mrs' by unmarried upper servants and elderly spinsters in order to increase their authority and credibility.

39. K. Everett, *Bricks and Flowers*, 1949.

40. 'Society is to the daughters of a family, what business is to the son'. Mrs Ellis, *Daughters of England*, 1842, p. 255. In her first season in 1849, Lady Dorothy Neville went to 50 balls, 60 parties, 30 dinners and 25 breakfasts. R. Neville (ed.), *The Reminiscences of Lady Neville*, 1909.

41. The banishment of boys to boarding schools kept them away from the

social arena at the awkward time when they were too old to be controlled at home but too young for full participation.

42. There is an excellent discussion of this effect on girl's education in J. Duguid Milne, *The Industrial and Social Position of Women in the Middle and Lower Ranks*, 1857.

43. Louisa Kathleen Haldane, *Friends and Kindred: Memoirs*, 1961, p. 95.

44. The meaning of this to the girl is captured in Rosamund Lehman's short novel, *Invitation to the Waltz*, 1932.

45. The Hon. Mrs Gell, *Under Three Reigns 1860–1920*, 1927, p. 49.

46. Marchioness of Londonderry, *Retrospect*, 1938.

47. G. Huxley, *Lady Denman, G.B.E., 1884–1954*, 1961, p. 24.

48. A. Freeling, *The Bride's Book: Being Hints for Regulating the Conduct of Married Women*, 1865.

49. Emily Charlotte Langtry, *The Days I Knew*, 1925, p. 104.

50. J. A. and O. Banks, *Feminism and Family Planning in Victorian England*, 1964.

51. Mrs R. Niall, 'The Political Salon of Today', *Lady's Realm*, October 1909, p. 155.

52. There is a kindly but candid portrait of such a mother in Noel Streatfeild's *A Vicarage Family*, 1963. See also 'Revolt of the Daughters', *Housewife's Magazine*, April 1903.

53. R. Neville, *The Reminiscences of Lady Dorothy Neville*, 1909.

54. The importance of commercial exploitation of these new social needs should not be overlooked but they are not enough to explain their origin or survival. A. Adburgham, 'The Apparel of Grief', in *Shops and Shopping 1800–1914*, 1964.

55. Certain materials like plush, velvet and satin could never be worn for mourning.

56. 'Mourning', *Sylvia's Home Journal*, February and September, 1881.

57. Nancy Mitford, *The Ladies of Alderley*, 1967, quoted in John Morley, *Death, Heaven and the Victorians*, 1921, p. 70.

58. While not going as far as Shils and Young in seeing such occasions as 'a great act of national communion', undoubtedly they did strengthen feelings of belonging to a community held together by 'family' bonds. Edward Shils and Michael Young, 'The Meaning of the Coronation', *Sociological Review*, December, 1953.

59. K. Woodroofe, *From Charity to Social Work in England and the United States*, 1962, pp. 54–55. G. Stedman Jones, *op. cit.* chapter 13.

60. Richard Doyle, *Bird's Eye View of Society*, 1864, p. 18.

CHAPTER IV—CHANGE AND DECLINE

1. A. Trollope, *The Way We Live Now*, 1875.

2. H. Perkin, *Origins of Modern English Society 1780–1880*, 1969.

3. Adapted from Ralph Pumphrey, 'The Introduction of Industrialists into the British Peerage', *American Historical Review*, p. 9.

4. Lord Ernest Hamilton, *The Halcyon Era*, 1933.

5. The fall in the middle-class birth-rate starting in the 1870s would have made itself felt by the end of the century creating more openings even if the parameters of 'Society' had not enlarged. Interests among the peers created included: railways, armaments and machinery, publishing, chemicals, textiles, mining, building and brewing.

6. Pumphrey, op. cit.

7. G. Huxley, *Lady Denman, C.B.E., 1884–1954*, 1961.

8. A. Glynn, *Elinor Glynn—A Biography*, 1955, p. 64.

9. G. Huxley, *Both Hands: An Autobiography*, 1970, p. 118.

10. 'The Enlargement of London "Society",' *Saturday Review*, May 5th, 1900.

11. See 'On the significance of numbers for Social Life: Aristocracies' in Kurt Wolff (ed.), *The Sociology of George Simmel*, 1950.

12. W. Mallock, 'The Basis of London Society', op. cit.

13. D. S. Peel, *Life's Enchanted Cup*, op. cit.

14. 'A Shady Social Enterprise', *The Realm*, March 8th, 1895.

15. Personal information.
For example in 1910 a new periodical appeared with the title, *The Green Book of London Society: being a directory of the Court, of Society and of the political and official world; including celebrities in Art, Literature, Science and Sport.*

16. B. Webb, *My Apprenticeship*, 1928, Penguin, Harmondsworth, p. 68.

17. T. H. Escott, *Social Transformation of the Victorian Age*, 1897, p. 90.

18. J. M. Lee, op. cit.

19. E. Adam (ed.), *Mrs J. Comyn-Carr's Reminiscences*, 1925, p. 27.

20. Lady Muriel Beckwith, *When I Remember*, 1936, p. 219.

21. Harold MacFarland '£.s.d. of a London Season', *Lady's Realm*, May 1909, p. 74.

22. Lady St Helier, *Memories of Fifty Years*, 1909.

23. Cynthia Asquith, *Remember and Be Glad*, 1952.

24. Lady Violet Hardy, *As It Was*, 1958, p. 107.

25. Lady Muriel Beckwith, *When I Remember*, 1936, p. 248.

26. Ursula Bloom, *Sixty Years of Home*, 1960.

27. Member of the Aristocracy, *Party Giving on Every Scale: or the Cost of Entertaining with the Fashionable Modes of Arrangement*, 1882.

28. Mrs Peel, *The Way We Lived Then 1914–1918, A Sketch of Social and Domestic Life in England During the War*, 1929.

29. Vera Brittain, *Testament to Youth*, 1933.

30. Beckwith, op. cit., p. 134.

31. P. Balfour, *Society Racket—A Critical Survey of Modern Social Life*, 1933.

32. W. Guttsman, op. cit., 1963.

33. J. Ellis, op. cit., 1962.

34. Their children, however, were often integrated via public schools and in any case, the increasingly middle-class background of labour leaders has created different problems for the Labour movement.

35. M. Cole, *Beatrice Webb*, 1945.

CHAPTER V—VARIATIONS: ANTI-SOCIETY AND EXTRA-SOCIETY

1. M. Stocks, *My Commonplace Book*, 1970, p. 24.

2. Mrs Gell, op. cit., 1927, p. 84.

3. And is inimitably sketched in Mrs Gaskell's *Cranford*.

4. Mrs Oliphant, *Miss Marjoribanks*, 1865, 1969.

5. Asa Briggs discusses some of the variations between local scenes in *Victorian Cities*, 1963. A good account of such a locally oriented family is Anne Vernon's *Three Generations: The Fortunes of a Yorkshire Family*, 1966.

6. J. Duguid Milne, op. cit., 1875.

7. A. Swan, *My Life: An Autobiography*, 1934.

8. By which the poor were increasingly isolated in the city centre. 'The rise of the middle class suburbs in which geographical insularity was often a symbol of a more fundamental social and political separation', H. J. Dyos, *Victorian Suburb: A Study of the Growth of Camberwell*, 1961, p. 25.

9. J. M. Richards, *Castles on the Ground*, 1946.

10. James Kenward, *The Suburban Child*, 1955.

11. Ronald Carton, *The Gentle Adventure: A Victorian Prelude*, 1933.

12. W. MacQueen-Pope, *Back Numbers: A Disturbance of the Dust of Yesteryear*, 1954, p. 28.

13. Katherine Chorley, op. cit.

14. R. Scott, *Elizabeth Cadbury 1850–1951*, 1955, A. Arnott, *The Brethren: An Autobiography of a Plymouth Brethren Childhood*, 1969. Even the Evangelicals had their annual May Meetings at Exeter Hall which 'became a powerful institution drawing country Evangelicals to London'. G. R. Balleine, *A History of the Evangelical Party in the Church of England*, 1908, p. 146.

15. L. E. O. Charlton (ed.), *The Recollections of a Northumbrian Lady 1815–1866*, 1949.

16. W. Mallock, op. cit., p. 97.

17. D. Hopkinson, *The Incense Tree, An Autobiography*, 1968.

18. H. E. M. Stutfield, *The Sovranty* [sic.] *of 'Society'*, 1909.

19. Acceptance of these minority groups through the formal hierarchic system of English 'Society' can be contrasted to the American black-balling of Jews, Negroes and other ethnic groups. These groups formed

their own imitations of 'Society' with their own season and their own leaders. See Appendix.

20. Robert Michels, *Political Parties: A Sociological Study of the Oligarchical Tendencies of Modern Democracy*, Glencoe Illinois, 1915. p. 261.

21. N. Annan, 'The Intellectual Aristocracy' in J. Plumb, *Studies of Social History*, 1955.

22. E. M. Forster, *Marianne Thornton: A Domestic Biography 1797–1887*, 1956.

23. W. J. Reader, op. cit.

24. Michael Holroyd, *Lytton Strachey: A Critical Biography*, 1967.

25. Mary Stocks, 'The Rendel Connection', *My Commonplace Book*, 1970; Gwen Raverat, *Period Piece*, 1952.

26. M. H. Watt, *The History of the Parson's Wife*, 1943. There are a great many reminiscences by clergymen's wives and daughters. Two that clearly bring out this dilemma, one in London and one in Glasgow are: E. Ballie, *The Shabby Paradise, the Autobiography of a Decade*, 1959; Anna Buchan, *Unforgettable, Unforgotten*, 1945.

27. A. Stirling, *Victorian Sidelights: From the papers of the late Mrs Adams Acton*, 1954.

28. 'Bohemians and Bohemianism', *Cornhill Magazine*, February 1865, p. 241.

29. W. H. Armytage, *Heavens Below, Utopian Experiments in England*, 1560–1960, 1961.

30. Edward Carpenter, *My Days and Dreams: Being Autobiographical Notes*, 1916. A similar but later experience is found in G. Brenan, *A Life of One's Own: Childhood and Youth*, 1962.

31. Charles Hart, 'Courtship and Marriage in the Novels of Anthony Trollope', Columbia University, unpublished Ph.D. thesis, 1968.

32. K. Chorley, op. cit., 1950. Upper-class families also seem to have given their dogs extreme license, possibly in compensation for the restraints on their own behaviour.

33. P. Cominos, 'Late-Victorian Sexual Respectability and the Social System', *International Review of Social History*, Vol. 18, 1963. Upper-middle class attitudes to the attempts at gentility were, as expected, patronising. T. H. Crosland, *The Suburbans*, 1905. A recent critic has noticed with surprise that we no longer find George Grossmith's *Diary of a Nobody* very funny. Perhaps that is because the whole system of defining a 'somebody' has withered away.

34. For a discussion of this point in a wider context see: Eve Sullerot, *Woman, Society and Change*, 1971.

35. How to Behave, op. cit., p. 96.

36. *The Life of Lily Langtry, the Jersey Lily and Queen of the Stage*, 1882.

37. A. L. Rowse (ed.), *A Cornish Waif's Story: An Autobiography*, 1954. The

institutions for 'saving' girls and women like Refuges and Penitentiaries in fact served to reinforce the labelling implied by the categories fallen and respectable. For a sociological explanation of such a device see: Stephen Box, *Deviance, Reality and Society*, 1971.

38. Those few who tried to bring the issues in front of middle-class audiences were not allowed a hearing. See Bernard Shaw's *Mrs Warren's Profession* (1894).

39. Which was one of its great attractions: S. Marcus, *The Other Victorians*, 1966; D. Fielding, *The Duchess of Jermyn Street: The Life and Good Times of Rosa Lewis*, 1964.

40. *Reformatory and Refuge Journal*, later called *Seeking and Saving*.

41. H. Ware, 'The Recruitment, Regulation and Role of Prostitution in Britain from the Middle of the 19th Century to the Present day', University of London, unpublished Ph.D. thesis, 1969.

42. The attacks in the press about the dress and behaviour of the 'Girl of the Period' in the 1860s stemmed from the fear that lines of respectability were becoming blurred.

43. Richard Deacon, *The Private Life of Mr Gladstone*, 1954.

44. G. J. Melville-Whyte, *Good for Nothing or All Down Hill, c.* 1900, p. 83.

45. Between 1818 and 1914, 17 million people left the British Isles— although many of these were emigrants, many also returned. F. Musgrove, *The Migratory Elite*, 1963.

46. Diana Black, *The Foot of the Rainbow*, 1961; E. M. Forster, *Passage to India*, 1924.

47. HMSO, *New Horizons, 100 years of Women's Emigration*, 1963.

48. It would be necessary to reconstruct a comparative cost of living scale to prove this point. However, numerous autobiographies refer to the relative simplicity of continental life in such a way that it seems to have been a case of relative rather than absolute difference in expenditure. M. Belloc-Lowndes, *I Too Have Lived In Arcadia*, 1942. L. E. Jones, *A Victorian Boyhood*, 1955.

49. Annabel Huth Jackson, *A Victorian Childhood*, 1932, p. 179.

50. G. Grigson, *The Crest on the Silver: An Autobiography*, 1950, p. 44.

51. E. M. Forster, *Marianne Thornton—Domestic Biography 1797–1887*, 1956.

CHAPTER VI—WOMEN AND WORK

1. Further research on this subject should be connected with the present discussion of deference and deferential behaviour. E. Goffman, 'The Nature of Deference and Demeanor', *American Anthropologist*, June 1956.

2. There is no intention to minimise the importance of the supply factor in housing and domestic service. For example, landlords had an interest in

continuing to rent property rather than sell it. There was a large surplus of female labour from the countryside, most of which went into service. But both supply *and* demand factors have to be taken into account when assessing the total situation.

3. After 1880, even country houses were rented rather than bought. M. Girouard, *The Victorian County House*, 1971.

4. L. E. O. Charlton (ed.), *The Recollections of a Northumbrian Lady, 1815–1866*, 1949, p. 263.

5. W. S. Clarke, *The Suburban Homes of London, A Residential Guide*, 1881.

6. The author of 'From Kitchen to Garret', *Leaves from a Housekeeper's Book*, (1st ed. 1887), 11th edition, 1914.

7. Katherine Furse, *Hearts and Pomegranates: The Story of 45 Years 1875–1920*, 1940.

8. R. Kerr, *The Gentleman's House or How to Plan English Residences from the Parsonage to the Palace*, 1864. The architectural segregation of various categories of prisoner or inmate by sex, age and type of offence began in the late eighteenth century. This concept was applied in workhouses, hospitals, orphanages and Rescue Homes as well as prisons. The rationale may have been a moral one but the effect was a much tighter control over inmates.

9. And smelling. Victorian architectural writers are obsessed with the fear of cooking smells pervading the halls or living-rooms in any way and go to elaborate ends to prevent this intrusion.

10. The influence of settings for social rituals, including the idea of a front and backstage is discussed in E. Goffman, *The Presentation of Self in Every Day Life*, 1959.

11. Several wealthy areas of London had gates across what were in effect private roads. This was a privilege vigorously contested by the city authorities.

12. The use of spatial arrangements to control accessibility is discussed in D. Smith, *Household Space*, MS, Department of Anthropology and Sociology, University of British Columbia, 1969.

13. A. W. Stirling *Life's Little Day: Some Tales and Other Reminiscences*, 1924.

14. A Lady in Society, *The New Book of Etiquette*, n.d.

15. 'Member of the Aristocracy', *The Management of Servants*, n.d., was written specifically as an introduction to the author's *Manners and Tones of Good Society*.

16. Paul and Thea Thompson, op. cit., interview.

17. M. Powell, *Below Stairs*, 1969; J. Rennie, *Every Other Sunday, The Autobiography of a Kitchen Maid*, 1955; C. Meyer 'The Servant Problem', *Occupational Psychology*, 1939.

18. An early nineteenth-century prosperous merchant's wife in London kept

a double entry 'account' of all visits paid and visits received, dinners given, dinners attended with the names of visitors recorded for each occasion. All these are neatly totalled by the month and by the year so that a complete social record was kept and progress noted in the most businesslike way. It is interesting to note that this couple moved from their home near the business in Limehouse to more socially acceptable Walthamstow when they must have been in early middle age. Mary Young, *Commonplace Book*, 1828–1840, 300.01 48. 85/3, London Museum Library.

19. B. Webb, *My Apprenticeship*, 1926, p. 71.

20. B. Frankle, op. cit., 1969.

21. W. H. Corfield, *Dwelling Houses: Their Sanitary Construction and Arrangement*, 1898. Even in the interwar period it was considered 'vulgar' to have hand basins in the bedroom rather than washstands with jugs and bowls to be filled and emptied by maids. (Personal information.)

22. One of the first labour-saving steps advised was painting all brass door furniture black. R. K. Phillips, *The Servantless House*, 1920; Mrs J. G. Fraser, *First Aid to the Servantless*, Cambridge, 1913; C. Buckton, *Comfort and Cleanliness: The Servant and the Mistress Question*, 1898.

23. B. Askwith, *Two Victorian Families*, 1971, p. 23.

24. Mary Wylde, *A Housewife in Kensington*, 1937.

25. Enid Starkie, *A Lady's Child*, 1941, p. 258.

26. E. Bancroft-Davis, *Letters from England, 1846–1849*, 1904, p. 28.

27. M. Taylor, *The First Duty of Women*, 1870, p. 51, quoted in J. and O. Banks, op. cit., p. 74.

28. M. L. Eyles, *The Woman in the Little House*, 1922.

29. Robert Dreeben, 'American Schooling: Patterns and Processes of Stability and Change' in B. Barber and A. Inkles (eds.), *Stability and Social Change*, Boston, 1971, p. 109.

30. Ernest King (as told to Richard Viner), *The Green Baize Door*, 1963, p. 39.

31. Lady Tweedsmuir, op. cit., p. 79.

32. Elinor Glynn never referred to her exceptionally successful and money-making novels as her work. For her, 'work' meant fancy embroidery or worsted work as it did to most Victorian women. A. Glynn, *Elinor Glynn— A Biography*, 1955.

33. Elizabeth Banks, 'Paying Occupations for Gentlewomen', *Cassell's Family Magazine*, April, 1896.

34. Letter to the editor of *The Englishwoman's Journal*, Vol. viii, 1866, p. 59.

35. Emma, Countess of Brownlow, *The Eve of Victorianism: Reminiscences of the Years 1802–1834*, 1940.

36. Dorothy Strachey, *Olivia*, quoted in B. Askwith, *Two Victorian Families*, 1971, p. 37.

37. Cecil Woodham-Smith, *Florence Nightingale, 1820–1910*, 1950.

38. Diana Hopkinson, *Family Inheritance: A Life of Eva Hubback*, 1954, p. 67.
39. Maisie Ward, *Unfinished Business*, 1964, p. 45.
40. Mary McCarthy, *A Nineteenth Century Childhood*, 1924, p.79.
41. Brian Harrison, 'Family, Church and Social Class in Late-Victorian England', (forthcoming) *Past and Present*.
42. This extract is probably based on first-hand experience. Emily Eden kept house for her brother when he was First Lord of the Admiralty and later when he became governor of India. Emily Eden, *The Semi-Attached Couple*, 1860, p. 125.
43. Virginia Woolf, *To the Lighthouse*, 1927, Penguin, Harmondsworth, p. 96.
44. Chester Kirby, *The English Country Gentleman: A Study of 19th Century Types*, c. 1925, pp. 111–112.
45. Margaret Fletcher, *O, Bring Back Yesterday*, 1939.
46. E. M. Delafield, *Diary of A Provincial Lady*, 1930, p. 140.
47. Lord Chamberlain, 'Presentation at Court' mimeo., 1958.
48. A few Oxbridge Colleges, the Diplomatic Corps and the monarchy in its public performances are the only centres where the rituals of etiquette are still taken seriously.
49. 'So What's Happened to the Season?', *Sunday Times*, October, 1971. L. Stanley, *The London Season*, 1955.

APPENDIX—SOCIETY IN TWO OTHER CULTURES

1. An Englishwoman married to a Russian gives a sketch of such a household, E. M. Almedingen, *Life of Many Colours—The Story of Grandmother Ellen*, 1958.
2. E. Digby Baltzell, *Philadelphia Gentlemen: The Making of a National Upper Class*, 1958.
3. Oliver Jensen, *The Revolt of American Women*, New York, 1952.
4. Personal information. For Chicago see Harvey Zorbaugh, *The Gold Coast and the Slum*, Chicago, 1920.
5. Rev. J. H. Ingraham, *Not 'A Fool's Errand': Life and Experience of A Northern Governess in the Sunny South*, New York, 1854, p. 507.
6. Michael Astor, *Tribal Feeling*, 1963.

BIBLIOGRAPHY

The following bibliography is only intended to provide background reading. Specialised references will be found in footnotes attached to the text. In the footnotes, the place of publication is London unless otherwise indicated.

Adburgham, Alison, *A Punch History of Manners and Modes, 1841–1940*, Hutchinson, London, 1961.

Ariès, Philippe, *Centuries of Childhood: a social history of family life*, Alfred Knopf, New York, 1962.

Avery, Gillian, *Victorian People in Life and Literature*, Collins, London, 1970.

Banks, J. A., and Olive, *Feminism and Family Planning in Victorian England*, Liverpool University Press, Liverpool, 1964.

Banks, J. A., *Prosperity and Parenthood, a study of family planning among the Victorian middle-class*, Routledge and Kegan Paul, London, 1954.

Barber, Elinor, *The Bourgeoisie in 18th Century France*, Princeton University Press, Princeton, New Jersey, 1955.

Besant, Walter, *Fifty Years Ago*, Chatto and Windus, London, 1888.

Best, Geoffrey, *Mid-Victorian Britain, 1851–1875*, Weidenfeld and Nicolson, London, 1969.

Bloom, Ursula, *Sixty Years of Home*, Hurst Blackett, London, 1900.

Bovill, E. W., *English Country Life 1780–1830*, Oxford University Press, Oxford, 1962.

Briggs, Asa, 'The Language of "Class" in Early Nineteenth Century England' in Briggs, A. and Saville, J. (eds), *Essays in Labour History*, Macmillan, London, 1967.

Briggs, Asa, 'Middle-Class Consciousness in English Politics, 1780–1846', *Past and Present*, No. 9, 1957.

Briggs, Asa, *Victorian Cities*, Odhams Press, London, 1963, Pelican Books, 1968.

Brittain, Vera, *Testament to Youth*, Gollancz, London, 1933.

Burn, W. L., *The Age of Equipoise, a study of the mid-Victorian generation*, Allen and Unwin, London, 1964.

Burnett, John, *A History of the Cost of Living*, Penguin Books, London, 1969.

Burnett, John, *Plenty and Want, a social history of diet in England from 1815 to the present day*, Thomas Nelson, London, 1966, Pelican Books, 1968.

Burton, Elizabeth, *The Early Victorians At Home, 1837–1861*, Longmans, London, 1972.

Chesney, Kellow, *The Victorian Underworld*, Temple Smith, London, 1970.

Christie, O. F., *The Transition from Aristocracy 1832–1867*, London, 1927.

Cominos, P., 'Late-Victorian Sexual Respectability and the Social System', *International Review of Social History*, Vol. 18, 1963.

Crozier, D., 'Kinship and Occupational Succession', *Sociological Review*, 1965.

Davidoff, Leonore, 'The Employment of Married Women in England and Wales, 1850 to 1950', unpublished M.A. thesis, University of London, 1956.

Escott, T. H., *Social Transformations of the Victorian Age*, London, 1897.

Escott, T. H., *Society in the Country House*, London, 1907.

Frankle, Barbara, 'The Genteel Family: High Victorian Conceptions of Domesticity and Good Behaviour', unpublished Ph.D. thesis, University of Wisconsin, 1969.

Girouard, Mark, *The Victorian Country House*, Clarendon, Oxford, 1971.

Guttsman, W. L. (ed.), *The English Ruling Class*, Weidenfeld and Nicolson, London, 1969.

Guttsman, W. L., *The British Political Elite*, MacGibbon and Kee, London, 1963.

Hamilton, Lord Ernest, *The Halcyon Era*, John Murray, London, 1933.

Harrison, Brian, *Drink and the Victorians, the temperance question in England 1815–1872*, Faber and Faber, especially Chapters 2 and 14, London, 1971.

Harrison, Brian, 'Underneath the Victorians', *Victorian Studies*, March, 1967.

Harrison, J. F. C., *The Early Victorians 1832–51*, Weidenfeld and Nicolson, London, 1971.

Houghton, W. E., *The Victorian Frame of Mind*, Yale University Press, New Haven, 1957.

Jaeger, M. J., *Before Victoria*, Chatto and Windus, London, 1956.

Kirby, Chester, *The English Country Gentleman, a study of nineteenth century types*, J. Clarke & Co., London, n.d.

Lee, J. M., *Social Leaders and Public Persons: a study of county government in Cheshire since 1888*, Oxford, 1963.

Lochhead, Marion, *The Victorian Household*, John Murray, London, 1964.

Marcus, Steven, *The Other Victorians: a study of sexuality and pornography in mid-nineteenth century England*, Weidenfeld and Nicolson, London, 1966.

Milne, John Duguid, *Industrial and Social Position of Women in the Middle and Lower Ranks*, Longmans Green, London, 1857.

Morley, John, *Death, Heaven and the Victorians*, Studio Vista, London, 1971.

Murray, E. C. Grenville, *Under the Lens: Social Photographs*, London, 1883.

Musgrove, F., *The Migratory Elite*, Heinemann Educational Books, London, 1963.

Neville, R., *London Clubs*, London, 1911.

Neville, R., *The World of Fashion 1837–1922*, London, 1923.

Peel, D. S., *The Stream of Time 1805–1861*, John Lane, London, 1931.

Peel, D. S., *Life's Enchanted Cup, 1872–1933*, John Lane, London, 1933.

Perkin, Harold, *The Age of the Railway*, Panther Books, London, 1970.

Perkin, Harold, *The Origins of Modern English Society, 1780–1880*, Routledge and Kegan Paul, London, 1969.

Perrott, R., *The Aristocrats: A Portrait of Britain's Nobility and their Way of Life Today*, Weidenfeld and Nicolson, London, 1968.

Pinchbeck, Ivy, *Women Workers and the Industrial Revolution, 1750–1850*, Frank Cass, London, 1969.

Ponsonby, A., *The Decline of Aristocracy*, London, 1912.

Pumphrey, Ralph E., 'The Introduction of Industrialists into the British Peerage: a study in adaptation of a social institution', *American Historical Review*, October, 1959.

Quinlan, Maurice, *Victorian Prelude: a history of English manners 1700–1830*, New York, Columbia University Studies in English and Comparative Literature, no. 155, 1941.

Reader, W. J., *Professional Men, the rise of the professional classes in nineteenth century England*, Weidenfeld and Nicolson, London, 1966.

Sackville-West, Victoria, *The Edwardians*, L. and V. Woolf, London, 1930.

Sala, George, *Twice Round the Clock or the Hours of the Day and Night in London*, London, n.d.

Stanley, L., *The London Season*, Hutchinson, London, 1955.

Stevenson J. J., *House Architecture*, Vol. II, London, 1880.

Stutfield, H. E. M., *The Sovranty* [sic.] *of Society*, London, 1909.

Thompson, F. M. L., *English Landed Society in the Nineteenth Century*, Routledge and Kegan Paul, London, 1963.

Webb, Beatrice, *My Apprenticeship*, Longmans Green, London, 1926, Penguin Books, 1971.

White, Cynthia L., *Women's Magazines, 1693–1968*, Michael Joseph, London, 1970.

Wildeblood, J., and Brinson, P., *The Polite World—A Guide to English Manners and Deportment From the Thirteenth to the Nineteenth Century*, Oxford University Press, Oxford, 1965.

Woodham-Smith, Cecil, *Florence Nightingale 1820–1910*, Constable, London, 1950.

ACKNOWLEDGEMENTS

· ❀ ·

The Publishers wish to thank the following for permission to use copyright photographs:

The Mansell Collection, 1; Radio Times Hulton Picture Library, 2, 4, 5, 6, 7, 8, 9, 11, 15, 16, 17, 19, 20, 21, 22, 23, 24, 25, 28, 29, 30, 32, 33, 36, 38; Punch, 3; R. H. Russell, 10, 26, 27, 31, 37; The Royal Photographic Society, 18, 34, 35; Hurlington Club, 43; The Croquet Association, 39; W. G. Davies, 40; Royal Institute of British Architects, London, 12; The Trustees of the British Museum, front and back end papers; The India Office Library, 13 and 14.

INDEX